CAMBRIDGE LIBRARY COLLECTION

Books of enduring scholarly value

Spiritualism and Esoteric Knowledge

Magic, superstition, the occult sciences and esoteric knowledge appear regularly in the history of ideas alongside more established academic disciplines such as philosophy, natural history and theology. Particularly fascinating are periods of rapid scientific advances such as the Renaissance or the nineteenth century which also see a burgeoning of interest in the paranormal among the educated elite. This series provides primary texts and secondary sources for social historians and cultural anthropologists working in these areas, and all who wish for a wider understanding of the diverse intellectual and spiritual movements that formed a backdrop to the academic and political achievements of their day. It ranges from works on Babylonian and Jewish magic in the ancient world, through studies of sixteenth-century topics such as Cornelius Agrippa and the rapid spread of Rosicrucianism, to nineteenth-century publications by Sir Walter Scott and Sir Arthur Conan Doyle. Subjects include astrology, mesmerism, spiritualism, theosophy, clairvoyance, and ghost-seeing, as described both by their adherents and by sceptics.

Spiritism

Eduard von Hartmann (1842–1906) had expected to follow his father's military career, but an injury forced him to reassess his ambitions. Torn between music and philosophy, he settled on the latter and in 1869 published his first book, *The Philosophy of the Unconscious*, which proved a great success. Published in 1885 as the period saw an enormous rise in the popularity of spiritualism, this work attempts to give psychological explanations for all occult phenomena, including subjective delusions as well as 'objective' physical manifestations, without resorting to hypotheses of ghosts, demons or trickery. C. C. Massey, a leading theosophist and translator of the work, wrote, 'Now for the first time, a man of commanding intellectual position has dealt fairly by us as an opponent.' This work will appeal to anyone with an interest in the growth of spiritualism and the philosophical and metaphysical debates of the nineteenth century.

T0345384

Cambridge University Press has long been a pioneer in the reissuing of out-of-print titles from its own backlist, producing digital reprints of books that are still sought after by scholars and students but could not be reprinted economically using traditional technology. The Cambridge Library Collection extends this activity to a wider range of books which are still of importance to researchers and professionals, either for the source material they contain, or as landmarks in the history of their academic discipline.

Drawing from the world-renowned collections in the Cambridge University Library and other partner libraries, and guided by the advice of experts in each subject area, Cambridge University Press is using state-of-the-art scanning machines in its own Printing House to capture the content of each book selected for inclusion. The files are processed to give a consistently clear, crisp image, and the books finished to the high quality standard for which the Press is recognised around the world. The latest print-on-demand technology ensures that the books will remain available indefinitely, and that orders for single or multiple copies can quickly be supplied.

The Cambridge Library Collection brings back to life books of enduring scholarly value (including out-of-copyright works originally issued by other publishers) across a wide range of disciplines in the humanities and social sciences and in science and technology.

Spiritism

Eduard von Hartmann
Translated by C.C. Massey

CAMBRIDGE UNIVERSITY PRESS

Cambridge, New York, Melbourne, Madrid, Cape Town,
Singapore, São Paolo, Delhi, Mexico City

Published in the United States of America by Cambridge University Press, New York

www.cambridge.org
Information on this title: www.cambridge.org/9781108052719

© in this compilation Cambridge University Press 2012

This edition first published 1885
This digitally printed version 2012

ISBN 978-1-108-05271-9 Paperback

SPIRITISM:

BY

EDUARD VON HARTMANN

Author of "The Philosophy of the Unconscious," &c.)

———

[Reprinted from " Light."]

———

PRICE THREE SHILLINGS.

——————

LONDON: THE PSYCHOLOGICAL PRESS,
16, Craven Street, Strand.

CONTENTS.

TRANSLATOR'S PREFACE.

The author of this pamphlet needs no introduction to the already large and increasing number of English readers who interest themselves in philosophy and its problems. He has almost certainly the widest influence on speculative thought in Germany of any contemporary writer. In this country his great work—though it has had later developments—has become accessible to a larger circle of readers through the recent translation by Mr. Coupland, of its ninth edition. The extensive acquaintance with the principles and results of modern science, which Dr. von Hartmann combines with high philosophical capacity, must impart to his opinions additional interest and authority. In this respect he is comparable to our own eminent philosopher, Mr. Herbert Spencer.

But however distinguished the author, to many it will seem that the subject of his present intellectual undertaking requires some apology. It is really in this very circumstance that the justification is to be found. The disregard of facts which only ignorance can any longer honestly deny, and which, whatever their true significance, must stand in important relation to very deep problems, is hardly less than scandalous to the thought and science of the age. However long this may have been felt and said, it would still seem presumptuous for any individual unsustained by authority to pronounce such a judgment. But the authority has recently become so imposing as indeed almost to remove the reproach itself. In this country, the Society for Psychical Research, an embodiment of the sentiment referred to,* has, within the last three years drawn to its ranks, and within its governing body, some of the most eminent representatives of science, philosophy, and literature. The number

---

* I do not by this mean to imply that this Society is already committed to the so-called Spiritualistic phenomena. That is not the case.

of its members and associates has been steadily increasing, similar societies are even now in course of formation, under the best leadership, in other countries, and less organised attempts in the same direction are engaging the energies of competent investigators in many quarters. From the public Press, representing the older and still dominant culture of the "Aufklärung," with its virtual denial of everything which could not be at once explained, or its shallow attempts to refer every phenomenal mystery to credulity and fraud, there has been little or no encouragement. Everything, on the contrary, which could discredit a subject peculiarly exposed to discredit has been eagerly seized upon, while the weighty evidence, which only students of the subject knew, they were seldom allowed to bring forward, except in books which were scarcely ever reviewed, and therefore remained unknown and unread by the public. Journals and periodicals there were, devoted to collection and discussion of the evidence as it arose, but these, again, were not allowed fair play. The great firm, for instance, which has the monopoly of the sale of literature to the travelling public, has never allowed any paper or book dealing with this subject to be exhibited on its stalls, nor will it even supply them to order. Papers ministering to the vulgarest frivolity of the populace are displayed, but such a journal as "LIGHT," for which the following translation was expressly prepared by authority of one of the most influential thinkers of the age, is not respectable enough for the fastidious vendors of *Rare Bits*, *Tit Bits*, and *Bird o' Freedom*.* In short, there has been a general consent that "Spiritualism" should be hustled out of sight, or be referred to only in terms of contempt, or for display of journalistic wit and superiority to "superstition." Nor has this opposition been at all conciliated by attempts to discriminate facts from their spiritistic interpretation.

It is hardly a serious imputation on journalists that they are subject to the prevailing intellectual influences. Greater responsibility falls on those whose profession it is to welcome

---

* I hope I have not done injustice to these publications. I confess I have not studied them, but the titles are suggestive, and they are to be found on Messrs. Smith and Co.'s bookstalls.

every foundation of fact for the discovery or recognition of truth. It will be an historical reproach to the Royal Society that it refused a hearing to Mr. Crookes' paper "On the Experimental Investigation of a New Force," and to the British Association for the Advancement of Science that the admission of Professor Barrett's paper "On some Phenomena associated with Abnormal Conditions of Mind," actually led to a revision of the rules, with the object of preventing the Association from being similarly "compromised" in future.

In Germany, the prejudice was exasperated a few years ago by the publication, by the late Professor Zöllner, of the report of his systematic investigation with the medium, Henry Slade.* To great scientific attainments and capacity, Zöllner united a very sensitive disposition, and it seems probable that the literary and private persecution which ensued conduced to his premature death. Intellectually and morally opposed to more than one of the prevailing tendencies of thought and practice, he turned on his assailants with a polemic which was not free from asperity, and in which the different topics of controversy, connected in Zöllner's view by a common derivation of the pernicious influences he was contesting, were mixed up with more abstract disquisitions. This circumstance, it will be seen, is considered by Dr. von Hartmann somewhat to detract from Zöllner's value as a witness. That is, as 1 submit, a very unnecessary concession to an "invention of the enemy," that Zöllner was mad ! a report which was spread after his death with no better justification than the impossibility of otherwise impairing the cogency of his evidence for the phenomena of "Spiritism." It is emphatically denied and conclusively disproved by the testimony of well-known men who were in intimate correspondence with Zöllner up to the time of his death. I refer to the report in this place, as well because Hartmann's remark might be thought to give some possible colour to it, as also because it was stated as a fact by a German physiologist in the *Contemporary Review* a year or two ago. It is *absolutely baseless.*

In some of his investigations with Slade (subsequent, by

---

* See my translation, "Transcendental Physics," which can be obtained at the Psychological Press Association, 16, Craven-street, Charing Cross.

the bye, to the occurrences which drove Slade from this country, and with which Zöllner was fully and exactly acquainted), Zöllner was associated with the distinguished men of science, Wilhelm Weber and Fechner, who added their testimony to his. The first professional conjurer in Germany, Samuel Bellachini, after prolonged investigation with Slade, also declared, by formal affidavit, the facts he had witnessed to be inexplicable by the resources of his art.

It was about this time that the public exhibitions of the " magnetiser," Hansen, drew fresh attention to the long dormant subject of mesmerism. In Germany, France, and England, some men of science reverted to the old experiments of Braid, and while still denying the specific influence of mesmerism, acknowledged, as completely proved and exempt from charlatanry, the extraordinary effects producible by suggestion in the state called hypnotism. The important development of this branch of psychology by Dr. Fahnestock, in the United States of America—who gave the apt term, " Statuvolence"—is adverted to by Hartmann in the text.

The next fact experimentally established was "thought-transference," without physical contact, and, therefore, without the possibility of involuntary muscular suggestions ; the results of the Society for Psychical Research in this country being confirmed by the independent investigations of M. Richet, in Paris.

Meanwhile the psychology of the abnormal conditions termed in general " somnambulic " was being studied by philosophers. The recently published work " Die Philosophie der Mystik," by Dr. Carl du Prel, of Munich, has the merit, quite apart from the author's theory of individual transcendental subjectivity, of showing the psychological continuity of the various states of sleeping consciousness, from ordinary dream to the wonderful faculties revealed by speech and action in the deepest somnambulic trance, as also the connection of these subjective phenomena with some occasionally observed in delirium and insanity. The discovery of this continuity and connection makes entirely credible, and even à priori probable, the statements of many medical observers of somnambulic patients,* which have

---

* Selections of this evidence will be found in du Prel's work, of which I have nearly completed a translation, to be published, I hope, before long.

long been ignored or rejected as incredible, by one side, while by another they have been accepted as demonstrating a world of spirits. Profoundly interesting is du Prel's exposition of this second consciousness in man, familiar to all in its weakest degree as common dream, but rising in clearness, coherence, and intensity in exact proportion as the organ of waking consciousness is numbed, and its functions are suppressed.

Another writer of philosophical repute in Germany, noted for his investigations of mediumistic phenomena, is Baron Lazar B. Hellenbach. His experience and conclusions are embodied in a work published at about the same time as du Prel's, entitled "Geburt und Tod als Wechsel der Anschanungsform oder die Doppel-natur des Menschen" (Birth and Death; as Change of Perceptional Form; or the Double-nature of Man). His hypothesis of a "Meta-organism" is allowed by Hartmann (who, nevertheless, considers it very improbable) to make the survival of the individual, after physical dissolution, scientifically conceivable.

The permissible space of a preface would be much exceeded by the enumeration of all, even of the more notable, indications that the dominant prejudice has failed to arrest observation and recognition of phenomena which are, indeed, of constant and natural recurrence. Sooner or later the human mind emancipates itself from the tyranny of intellectual conventionality, and the process is quickened when leaders of thought, like the author of this pamphlet, are in open sympathy with the revolt.

To gain the subject in hand a hearing, that public recognition of the value of study and research in it may be the sooner arrived at, is one object I have had in view in undertaking this translation. Hartmann's demand for State-appointed commissions of investigation is more appropriate to conditions of scientific research in Germany than to those obtaining in this country. Nor otherwise is it a very hopeful proposal. For success in this inquiry those who undertake it should in general be qualified by sympathies and interests intimately concerned in the elicitation of the phenomena. The mere physicist, or physiological psychologist, is too little likely to touch the springs of the subtle forces which are liberated by mental, though not always conscious dispositions. The recognition of a relatively unconscious mentality, in connection with the organic forces which are certainly in-strumental, suffices to bring into view the peculiar difficulties of the investigation. It would be the grossest mistake to assume, however, that only emotional and uncritical partisans of mediums are therefore likely to meet with a success which they would thus be unqualified to verify satisfactorily for others. But the demand for scientific examination of this subject usually assumes that nothing more is requisite than habits of observation and acute-ness acquired in physical experimentation. Yet it is quite likely that of two men equally qualified by such training, one shall have uniform success, and the other uniform disap-pointment with mediums. A very strong professional medium, through whom certain habitual phenomena are regularly elicited, may still obtain them without the assistance of *rapport*, that is, with quite neutral visitors, but a hostile will, however disguised, can paralyse the medium's forces, or deflect them in the possibly com-promising direction which, by expecting, it in fact dictates. This applies to the suspicion of prejudice, but not to the suspicion, if such it can be called, of wary and critical observation by a fair mind. Thus sinister suspicion is very frequently gratified by the result, if any result at all there is ; and this I believe to be the true explanation of some notable "exposures." People who cannot recognise in mental dispositions positive forces, acting by irresistible mesmeric suggestion upon a sensitive subject, have no business with experiments in which the psychological factor pre-dominates. Least of all is this factor to be ignored in the case of investigators of remarkable distinction, because the very force of character which has conduced to success in their own depart-ments of activity makes it unlikely that they will be psychically passive or neutral witnesses.

It is accordingly to be hoped that there will be no such scientific commissions as Dr. von Hartmann proposes, until these incidents of the research have become thoroughly understood. Voluntary organisations may be more effectual, because originat-ing in a genuine interest. But even in these success will be rather individual than collective, and it is probable that the best observations will not be those of committees selected chiefly on account of the authority their names would carry with the public. Such considerations are natural, but they ignore the fact that every member of the committee, as soon as he enters the séance-room, is a " psychic " only in a less degree than the medium himself, and should be a co-efficient in the results. Hartmann is undoubtedly right in asserting this co-efficiency, though it is of very various degrees, and is often not at all apparent. To these degrees of co-efficiency correspond degrees of counteracting influence, leading to failure or to questionable results. While I quite admit that professional mediumship has been disgraced by many conscious frauds, and must always be narrowly watched on account of the temptations offered by uncritical observation, it is my conviction that cruel injustice has often resulted from mere ignorance of psychological dynamics.

On the other hand, the author's theory of transferred and collective hallucinations at séances reverses the true position of the parties, making the medium stand to the others in the relation of mesmeriser to his subjects. It is, indeed, no logical answer to Hartmann that experienced investigators would unanimously disagree with him (who has here no experience) on this point, because the theory itself requires that the greater the experience, the greater are the probability and force of such psychological deceptions. But his analogies do not help him : hallucinations of all the senses, combined into a single object, perceived uninterruptedly for a length of time, and similarly by a number of observers, have not, I believe, been independently established. Nor is it easy to suppose that Mr. Crookes and his friends, for instance, were thus hallucinated by the little Florence Cook, to the extént described.

Nevertheless, the facts of somnambulism, and the field of psychology to which they introduce us in relation to mediumistic phenomena, have certainly been too much neglected by Spiritualists. Herein they have been neither more nor less wise than other people. As long as man's ideal life is supposed to be limited to the content of his waking consciousness, it is inevitable that whatever exceeds this content, either in the deeper states of dream or in communications obtained through mediums, should be ascribed to foreign intelligences. Only recently and partially has the organic " threshold " of consciousness been recognised, and the insight been gained that all which lies behind that threshold—the "unconscious cerebration of Carpenter—or the "latent thought" of Hamilton— is only not conscious in the sense that it has not attained the *reflective* moment of consciousness, and is thus not yet associated with the *self*-consciousness. How large, and in what relations with nature and other subjects, may be this unappropriated sphere of individual being, it must belong to a more mature metaphysic and psychology to determine. We have at present only to remember that Hartmann's postulate that the consciousness behind the normal threshold—or the "somnambulic" consciousness—is supported by a part of the brain whose functional activities are only "masked" by those of the parts supporting waking consciousness, is a mere physiological assumption. That the "unconscious" ideal processes go on during waking life, being indeed only "masked" by the impressions of the latter, is doubtless a fact sustained by presumption, analogy, and psychological evidence. But the "supporter" of this relatively unconscious or somnambulic ideality is entirely problematical. It may be a substance which we can represent organically, and which yet has no organic dependence on the brain, and may survive the disintegration of the latter, appropriating then the self-consciousness and personality of the individual. The intimate connection with the brain, or at least with some part of the physical organism,* which this hypothetical "meta-organism" must certainly have, is not necessarily, or even presumably, a relation of dependence. The recognition of finer forms of matter than can affect our physical sensibility must carry with it the possibility of their organic constitution, and this possibility may be raised to the rank of a necessary hypothesis by the more profound psychology for which somnambulism seems to offer a foundation.†

It must be a question for psychologists, if not for metaphysicians, whether Hartmann has not ascribed to the "masked" somnambulic consciousness (the ideal process behind, yet co-existing with, the waking consciousness), powers which, by the very laws

---

* Some somnambules have placed the seat of abnormal consciousness and its perceptions in the region of the solar plexus.

† On this whole subject du Prel's "Philosophie der Mystik" offers very instructive considerations.

of consciousness, can only belong either to the external or to the internal waking state ; that is, to ordinary self-conscious thought, or to the self-consciousness of "open" somnambulism. Analysis of consciousness yields two moments, the direct and the reflective. The latter, which is the recognition and characterisation of the thought—its "second intention," in the language of the schoolmen*—seems to be essential for the motivation of all actions of apparent intelligence, other, that is, than the automatic actions which have merely reflex movements at their foundation. A thought unrecognised and unattached to the self-consciousness may indeed pass into an action appropriate to it (as in the simplest phenomenon of planchette writing, &c.), and this ideo-motive process may go on spontaneously as long as it depends simply on the uninterrupted current of automatic thought behind the "threshold." But if, now, it becomes a question of a fresh process suggested *from without*, of *response*, for instance, to another intelligence, it is difficult to conceive this happening without the *second* moment of mentality, the *recognition* of meaning, by which alone, it seems, a responsive association of ideas could be started, and a new set of actions could be set up. If here that second moment of consciousness is really, as I submit, requisite, it is evident that for all the more advanced phenomena of this province Hartmann's "masked" somnambulism is nothing less than a contemporaneous second intelligence, wanting nothing that belongs to full self-conscious personality. It is a second Ego in no subjectively deficient sense of the word. For we cannot conceive the intelligent *recognition* of a thought unaccompanied by a self-consciousness. In "open" somnambulism we undoubtedly find this full intelligence, but in that state the ordinary physical Ego-consciousness is dormant.

I wish only to point out what is apparently involved in Hartmann's hypothesis that the "masked" somnambulic consciousness is competent to the ideal element in all phenomena occurring in the medium's waking state. In place of a spirit-Ego beyond the organism, he duplicates the physical Ego within the organism ; and that not in the sense in which du Prel,

‡ The distinction is admirably brought out and explained by Mr. Shadworth Hodgson, as well in his "Time and Space," as in his "Philosophy of Reflection,"

indeed, finds this duplication (or, as he calls it, " self-sunder-ing ") in the dream states, wherein the subjective activity from behind the normal threshold dramatises as *objective* agent merely in the dream life, but as a veritable co-existence of self-conscious personalities belonging to, and dependent on, the same physical organism. That our organic self-consciousness may be a mere conditioned limitation of a larger and truer self, in other words, that this consciousness does not exhaust the self, the individual, or that the " person " is not co-extensive with the "subject," is quite another proposition, of which Kant gave the first hint in modern philosophy, and which is du Prel's doctrine of transcendental subjectivity.

As regards the physical phenomena of mediumship, I think the opinion of most persons conversant with them will be that Hartmann s hypothesis is too complicated in itself, and even thus is inadequate to the facts. But as it is certain that some physical emanation from the medium determines the range and power of the agency, there seem to be but two alternatives to the dynamical system advocated in this pamphlet. One is the extra-organic duplication of the medium, in whole or in part, such that the phantom person or limb draws to itself the forces of the organism, which, or the corresponding member of which, is left cold and inanimate by the transfer. Thus, if the whole phantom were projected, the state of the medium at the table would be that of trance, as happens often, but by no means always, during the course of strong physical phenomena at a distance. The reunion with the organism—the "repercussion" —is instantaneous. This hypothesis (which has a great deal of authority and evidence in support of it) would show the futility of certain ingenious " exposures " of mediums by staining the so-called "spirit-hand " (or other part) with substances after-wards found on the corresponding part of the medium. For upon the rejunction, any such foreign matter would naturally be deposited on the surface of the medium's body. It is a good test to distinguish this case from the alternative one of "spirit" agency, but proves nothing necessarily against the integrity of the medium. Hartmann's remarks on the ignorance of "exposers" have an even wider application than he imagined.

The absence of any definite account of the process implied

in the above supposition must be admitted ;* yet it is not inconceivable, and it has evidence of direct observation in its favour.†

The other alternative is that the medium's "aura" or "atmosphere," supplies the condition within its circuit for the physical operation of the invisible agencies called spirits, which need not necessarily be human, or even with independent intelligence in the sense of rationality. The possibilities of Nature beyond the senses are infinite, and as there are mundane animals below humanity, it is an admissible conjecture that there is no grade of life without etherial representation.‡

The agency of human spirits has, I believe, been greatly exaggerated by Spiritualists, and most of the communications purporting to come from them are sufficiently explained by causes too little recognised. The current Spiritualist conception of death as a simple change of external conditions, so that there is a mere continuity of consciousness on the same level, and in the same modes, seems to me to denote great poverty of thought ; nor are we constrained to accept it on the evidence of facts. That true communications from deceased persons there are, I believe ; but if we consider that the indrawal of consciousness to a deeper subjective degree must needs be retarded by lingering affinities—it may be of affection, or it may be of sense—which detain the spirit, all unsuited as its conditions are, in earth-life and its memories, we shall find nothing in the facts appealed to by Spiritualists inconsistent with a finer and profounder doctrine of the soul than any external phenomena can reveal. It is very significant that the most urgent to communicate are seldom those who have passed away in the fulness of time, but rather suicides, victims of fatal accident, or such as have otherwise been prematurely deprived of their organic connection with earth-life.

The author has repudiated an *à priori* negation of the spirit

---

* See, however, on this point Hellenbach's "Geburt und Tod," &c. Vienna, 1885.

† Hartmann's references by no means exhaust the best authorities. The works of the American writer, Epes Sargent, should especially be consulted. See also D'Assier's "L'Humanité Posthume," (Paris, 1882) on the above point.

‡ I hope it will not be supposed that this is a suggestion of the survival of our animals as spirits, and of their agency at séances !

hypothesis,* and all, but especially admirers of his philosophical genius, must readily accept his disclaimer of a position which would only be appropriate to a materialist. But he certainly seems to confound, in one indiscriminate denunciation, belief in spirits and their agency with a revival of mediæval superstition in its grossest forms, or rather he assumes the latter to be an inseparable result of the former. Yet it was not the belief as such, but the ignorant connotations of the belief, that led to the worst consequences in former times. The worst superstition was that which led to the persecution of the superstitious. In the nature of things there is no reason why belief in spirits should not recover its place in human culture, or why the foundations of the belief should not be cleared from mischievous misconceptions by an enlightened study and research. That certainly was the opinion of the greatest of modern philosophers. "I confess," said Kant ("Träume eines Geistersehers," &c.), "that I am much disposed to assert the existence of immaterial natures in the world, and to place my own soul in the class of these beings." Nay, more : Kant even anticipated the empirical proof of this fact, the physical condition being, perhaps, a partial solution of the cellular organism, conditioning our normal sensibility, and masking one for subtler impressions. And, therefore, he says in the following passage that the proof is not forthcoming, "as long as all goes well," viz., as long as the physical integrity in which health consists is unimpaired, whereas it seems probable that in the abnormal persons called mediums and somnambules, some constitutional lesion has been either inherited or incurred, or there is some disturbance of nervous equilibrium. "It will hereafter, I know not where or when, yet be proved that the human soul stands even in this life in indissoluble association with all immaterial natures of the spirit world, that it reciprocally acts on these and receives impressions from these, of which as man it is not conscious, as long as all goes well." (Id.) The fact is that, as the German proverb runs, "the child has been shaken out with the bath." The old popular and theological belief in spirits was encrusted with conceptions from which intelligence has been progressively breaking loose for the last

* In a letter to me which has been published in the journal "LIGHT."

two centuries. Modern rationalism has not analysed or dis-
criminated. Facts of nature, clothed upon by ignorance and
religious superstition,* have been treated as equally subjective
with their investiture. Or rather, this having once happened, we
have now to rediscover, in an experience very perplexing to our
sophisticated intelligence, that there really is a nature beneath
the surface with which our senses connect us. A late American
writer† has suggested, with considerable probability, that the
wholesale destruction, by fanaticism, of the mediums and
somnambules,called witches in former generations, almost exter-
minated the germs of the abnormal natures which bring sub-surface
facts to observation. Ignorant persecution has thus, perhaps,rein-
forced the materialistic tendency of modern rationalism by a
long suppression of the evidence which would refute it. On the
other hand, unbelief has been favourable to the slow and
silent reproduction of the germ remnants, which have within
the last generation produced a crop that can no longer remain
unnoticed. "Mediumistic" persons are now undoubtedly mul-
tiplying in an extraordinary ratio, and it will be increasingly
difficult to ignore the resulting phenomena.

It is a favourite à priori argument against the recognition of
spirit agency that it is inconsistent with the progressive displacement of such agency by science. But it does not follow,
because general laws have been substituted for immediate
acts of will in the regular phenomena of the universe, that
no acts of will remain, to which psychological laws, indeed, but
only such, are applicable. Acts of will have appropriate phenomena, and we are not to ignore them because man has
formerly confounded the phenomena of physical nature with
the phenomena of psychical nature. If, however, the phenomena
in question are subject to physiological laws, and thus explainable, by all means let us have the information from
scientific research. It is all we ask. The plea is for research
and study ; that these methods should supersede a "con-
spiracy of silence" unworthy of human intellect and honesty.
Let there be an end to this conventional affectation, an

---

* Which still makes many of the clergy, in dealing with this subject, the
powerful allies of materialism.

† Epes Sargent.

B

end to the preposterous pretence that "Spiritualism" is not a subject which men of " culture" can touch ! Your " culture" may not touch it, but if not, it will very soon itself touch your " culture" at the very foundation ! Of that there are already many symptoms. Meanwhile, it is no doubt the fact that such part of the uncritical populace as has addicted itself to Spiritism has seen the agency of spirits in much that belongs to the province of ordinary psychology, or even to the common accidents of life. But these are not the representatives of the revival, but its *enfants terribles.* A much more educated and intelligent class, also, have perhaps erred, owing to imperfect acquaintance with the psychology of somnambulic states. But there has long been an increasing tendency to discrimination, combined with a tolerance and open-mindedness not, perhaps, to be discovered in any other movement that has appealed so profoundly to emotional interests. Dr. von Hartmann seems to have mistaken the first ebullition of the revival in Germany, where it is not ten years old, and its extravagances in America, where it was so rapidly disseminated that corrective influences are only now beginning to make themselves felt, for its true tendency. The fact that this translation was first published in the columns of the Spiritualist journal "LIGHT" perhaps sufficiently evidences the liberal disposition of Spiritualists in this country. I refer, of course, to the higher level of intelligence, according to which every school, or sect, or party should be judged. But as it is not to be denied that ignorant and unbalanced minds may take harm by contact with a subject condemned to intellectual neglect, yet offering experiences of extraordinary attraction, this consideration may well be urged in addition to that of the great scientific interests involved, upon those who can influence the directions which serious inquiry and discussion should take.

C. C. M.

SPIRITISM.

By Eduard von Hartmann.

I. The General State of the Question.

The word "Spiritism" is of French production, the English, and generally the Germans, having retained the term "Spiritualism;" but it seems advisable to confine the latter to the metaphysical position opposed to Materialism, and not confounding it with the explanation of mediumistic phenomena by the co-operation of spirits, to designate that explanation by the recent term "Spiritism." The preponderating tendency in Spiritism is the American-English, which does not accept Re-incarnation, but mainly proceeds upon the Christian belief in immortality. In France the direction given by Allan Kardec prevails, namely, the inclination to the Indian belief that the soul has to re-incarnate itself in new bodies till it has realised its divine aspiration for perfection. In Germany, Hellenbach's transcendental individualism has a circle of adherents who teach the possibility, but not quite the necessity, of Re-incarnation, and are chiefly distinguished from French Spiritism by attaching just as little importance to the utterances of mediums as that school attaches much.

The number of Spiritist journals is considerable; *Psychische Studien* exchanges with fifty of them, and in Germany alone there are five. Most of them are uncritical and superstitiously credulous to a really incredible degree, the worst of all in this respect being the American reports, their value being further reduced by the fact that it is just in America that the humbug and swindles of professional mediums have reached their climax. Among German Spiritist journals the monthly *Psychische Studien* (Leipzig: Oswald Mutze, 1874-1885) occupies an exceptional position, the conductor, Dr. Wittig, representing with energy and critical acumen Cox's theory of psychic force and the hallucination hypothesis against the spirit hypothesis, especially in the last three years. It is characteristic of the whole movement that this attempt to secure a hearing for the voice of reason, and to raise his journal to a scientific level, can only be carried out in conflict with the chief of the paper and the majority of the staff,* and that its first result has been the springing up of several competitive papers. For as most of the subscribers to Spiritist journals have no scientific interest whatever in the explanation of the phenomena, but only the interest of the heart in the confirmation of their belief in immortality by means of them, the deprivation of this hope is at once the cessation of their whole interest in the matter.

Whoever will concern himself with the literature of the Spiritists must take up the position of a physician of the insane, who obtains from his patients the exactest description possible of their delusions ; and he who has no patience to enter and become familiar with the circle of ideas and the typical modes of expression of this mental aberration will never fathom its psychological causes.

That a somnambule represents under an image, and as far as possible personifies, the ideas (*Vorstellungen*) of his middle-brain, is a psychological necessity over which as a somnambule he has no power. That a masked (*larvirter*) somnambule ascribes the intelligent manifestations of his somnambulic consciousness, which his ordinary consciousness does not recognise as his "own," to foreign, invisible, personified intelligences, is not less psychologically necessary. Now if, further, those activities by which the, to him, unconscious intelligence of his masked somnambulic consciousness mediates its manifestations, are produced by

---

* It is necessary to explain that though *Psychische Studien* is described on the title page as "edited and superintended" (*herausgegehen und redigirt*) by Alex. von Aksakow, and Dr. Wittig describes himself as "editorial secretary" (*Sekratar der Redaction*), the supremacy of the former seems merely nominal, but the latter seems to be the responsible conductor of the paper.—TR.

involuntary and unconscious impulse of his middle-brain (be
it on the muscles of the limbs or vocal organs, or upon a
still unknown nerve-force of mechanical agency), it is
inevitable that he should deny these activities to be his own,
and should look on them as immediate activities of those
personified intelligences. And if with these processes is
connected the faculty which the somnambule has of producing combined hallucinations of several sense-organs in
the souls of sensitive persons present, the latter will be
easily disposed, on account of the ' palpability " of these
combined hallucinations of sight, hearing, feeling, and
touch, to take them for objective realities. And if, finally,
the agreement of these implanted hallucinations is proved
by several witnesses, the reality of the phenomena seems to
them, as to the somnambule influencing them, scarcely to
admit of further doubt.

All these intuitive fallacies have the same conformity
to psychological law as deceptions of the senses. Abstract
reflection may completely see through a deception of sense,
without the latter ceasing to reproduce itself for perception
as often as the conditions of its origination recur. For part
of the mediumistic phenomena, especially the transfer of
hallucination to third persons, undisturbed belief in the
reality of the dream-personifications appears to be an
almost indispensable condition in the somnambule evoking
them, and to be at least favourable for effectuation in the
witnesses. This explains why spectators encounter more
developed phenomena with the growth of their spiritistic
faith, and how an *intolerant* scepticism, which disdains to
conform, even in appearance, to the ideas of the medium,
must have a paralysing action on the latter's productive
power.

From these preliminary remarks it will be already seen
that in the phenomenal province on which Spiritism
rests we have to do with essentially different conditions of
research than in experiments with inorganic substances or

organic bodies. A small part only of mediumistic phenomena is purely physical in its action, and even this part is connected in its origin with psychical conditions, with the disposition, confidence, and untroubled comfort of the medium. Now it is quite unwarranted for men of science to decline the examination of these phenomena because they are connected with conditions the re-establishment of which is not always in the power of the investigator.

If the flea of the mole, or the intestinal worm of the cricket is to be examined, moles and crickets must first be caught for the fleas and worms to be found. If particular forms of insanity are to be examined the madhouses where such patients are to be found must be visited. If electric roaches or eels are to be examined, they must be obtained from their resorts. Just in the same way, if we would study abnormal phenomena of human nature we must seek out abnormally disposed natures or get them to come to us. Even the experiments of the laboratory are often so dependent on complicated conditions that the investigator cannot answer for success in every case; but this does not impair the demonstrative force of successful cases. If the electric roach is exhausted by the journey or is sick, the experiments with it must be just as unsatisfactory as those with a medium who is unwell ; and if the dampness of the atmosphere exceeds a certain degree, experiments with an electrical friction machine will miscarry just as much as those with a medium. All this, however, cannot possibly prevent the investigation of abnormal phenomena.

Worse than the dependence on mediums and their disposition is the contest with intentional deception, which is certainly spared in the investigation with electric roaches. Here, however, we are reminded of the provinces of mental and nervous disease, hysteria and somnambulism, where the physician and the theorist have likewise to deal with the subtlest attempts at deception, without their scientific zeal being arrested on that account. A somnambule receives from his phantasmic personages directions which he punctually obeys, in the good faith that they are acting through him, and in his waking state swears with a good conscience that he knows nothing of those actions, holding them immediate performances of those figures of his phantasy. Similarly a medium in the somnambulic state can play the part of a spirit and do things of which afterwards, when awake, he knows nothing, and which from the reports of the witnesses he must take for immediate spirit actions.

Whoever has been closely concerned with hysterical patients, without being their dupe, knows how finely and intricately good faith and deceit are entwined in them. Now all such mediums as are not merely magnetisers but also open or masked somnambules, are without exception individuals with a certain disorganisation of the nervous system; that is, the lower and middle nerve centres are too independent of the highest, reflex-inhibiting centre of conscious self-control; they are, in other words, just as much as non-mediumistic somnambules, and notwithstanding frequent appearance of bodily health, hysterical;* and their actions, whether in open or in masked somnambulism, are thus under the most favourable conditions imaginable for unconscious or half-conscious deceit. They are firmly convinced that the spirits help them, but are yet conscious that they are in some way indispensable to the spirits as a co-operating condition, that is, that the spirits can only act with their help. Is it a great step from this to the endeavour, on their own side, to help the spirits, so that the boundary between wholly involuntary, half-voluntary, and voluntary co-operation gets obliterated? Can generally the conception of "full accountability" be applied to a mental condition in which the organic-psychical collective energy is split between waking consciousness and somnam-

---

* That hysteria is not merely a female disease has been considered established in France for twenty years, and in Germany has lately been placed beyond doubt by Mendel.

bulic consciousness, leaving for the first only a proportion, greater or less, of the normal intensity?

It must, I think, be of singular occurrence for a completely normal man to have the notion of coming out as a medium. The best qualified would evidently be conjurers, but these prefer to carry on their art before a larger circle of spectators, while to mediums are allotted the small profits of a narrow circle. One has heard, indeed, of many mediums who have become conjurers, but never of a conjurer who has become a medium. It may, therefore, be assumed that no one enters the career of a medium who has not accidentally discovered in himself abnormal properties and forces. Somewhat of these properties and forces may indeed belong to every one, but in so slight a degree that nothing special is to be done with them. In England 3 per cent. ; in America, where the air is dryer, even as many as 5 per cent. of people are mediums to an extent worth cultivation. With women the development of these abnormal dispositions is more frequent than with men, with lean, nervous constitutions more frequent than with the stout, with young persons more frequent than with older ones, before puberty more frequent than afterwards.

The medium at self-discovery is usually as much astonished by the phenomena as are those about him ; it requires long exercise so far to obtain control over his middle nerve centres as to be able voluntarily to place himself in the condition adapted to elicit the phenomena. As this exercise progresses, the phenomena increase in variety and strength, and his notoriety extends ; by-and-bye he receives invitations to other towns and countries, with guarantee of compensation. If before he has been stimulated by vanity, now pecuniary interest is added ; he neglects his ordinary calling and becomes a professional medium. It is disagreeable to him to accept money for unsuccessful sittings, and yet he must have money to live; he begins to help the spirits that so his customers may be satisfied.

The professional medium is paid for each sitting ; the more sittings, the more money. But every sitting is a tension to the nervous system, and makes the medium more nervous, more hysterical, more powerless. As long as youth's store of force holds out, the thing prospers ; then the exhausted mediumistic force abates considerably, and phenomena are rarer and weaker. But notoriety pursues him, and he has more invitations than he can accept ; he sees before him money which he cannot earn. Now is the temptation to help the spirits urgent. Scarcely any professional medium is spared this diminishing phase of his mediumship, and it needs great strength of character again to take up the abandoned ordinary occupation after long erratic life. Many mediums prefer to become anti-Spiritists, and to entertain the public with the tricks by which they formerly helped the spirits, earning thereby, as a rule, much more than by genuine mediumship. Thereby also particular mediumistic performances, which can be produced in larger circles (e.g., thought-reading by contact and by the involuntary muscular movements of the directive person) are further carried on, and the anti-Spiritism is only used to conciliate the requisite confidence ; the conjuring goes on at the same time, and the public is far more certainly duped by these anti-Spiritists than by the Spiritist mediums. Many mediums arrive at length at complete derangement of body and mind, become infirm or melancholy, and end in insanity or suicide. This is the case, not only with American mediums, but also with the Indian, although the latter can never make the thing pecuniarily profitable, and are far less tempted to exhaust their power by too frequent exercise ; but the Indian mediums aim at just that derangement of mind and body which our medicine fears, and see in the gradual decay and dying away before death the most desirable goal.

Between a conjurer and a medium an important distinction is perceivable. The conjurer is independent of his health, of atmospheric conditions, of the dispositions towards him of those present, of the number of spectators, and light; on the other hand, he is dependent on the locality, on appliances, on the distance and position of the spectators, and in m ost performances on the preparations he has been able to make. He is seldom without confederates, and he has not to reckon with nervous exhaustion from the representation; he is dependent on certain conditions, but if these are not disturbed he is as good as sure of success. All this is otherwise with the medium.

The medium comes alone, without assistants and without apparatus, into a place which is strange and not accessible to him before the sitting. The Indian fakir appears naked, with only a rag round his loins; every sensible medium—and none others should be experimented with—willingly allows himself to be searched from head to foot before and after the sitting, and does not refuse to exchange, under inspection, the clothes he has brought on him for others newly provided of particular cut and colour. Every article he needs is received from the host, so that any preparation before the sitting is excluded. During the sitting the medium is immediately under the eyes of the spectators and in contact with them; but as he is influenced by their ideas and feelings, a malevolent, hostile, or frivolous disposition disturbs his psychical activity, and that equally whether he is conscious of the reason of this disturbance or not. Since each brings different thoughts, feelings, and influences, the disturbing influences are multiplied with the numbers of the spectators; mediumistic representations in the presence of more than three are antecedently to be suspected, and are usually only successful when among the spectators are mediums, who unconsciously reinforce the principal medium, and thus compensate for the disturbing influences.

The nervous relaxation and exhaustion of the medium is

proportional to the abundance and strength of the results produced, but may, of course, be feigned or hypocritically exaggerated. Success is entirely uncertain, and if the medium is to be kept from all temptation to imposition, it must before all things be made clear to him that one is aware of this uncertainty of success, and will be in no way disappointed or impatient, though even many sittings should be without result. It is also to be recommended not to pay mediums for each sitting, but to arrange with them a fixed sum per month, or for a series of sittings, with free quarters, because with the fee for each sitting there is a powerful motive to deceptions.

Not less obstructive to mediumistic effects than damp air and evil disposition of the spectators, is the glaring light, which the conjurer prefers, so that it should not be thought that he was making things too easy for himself by darkness. Most mediums must first discover and develop their powers by dark sittings, till they are so far strengthened and inured as to be able to bear a moderate light. Only distinguished mediums succeed with full light ; certain results, as for instance the levitation (*Emporfliegen*) of the medium, and the implantation of hallucinations in the spectators, seem under all circumstances to endure only a subdued light. As certainly as the different forms of the electric glimmer can only be observed in the dark chamber, so certainly also the phosphorescent lights, which are very common attendant phenomena of dark sittings, can only be witnessed in the dark. It is, therefore, impracticable to reject dark sittings altogether. Yet they should be confined to the study of these phenomena, and no value should be attributed to anything else occurring in them. Sleeves, boots, and cap of the medium, as perhaps other objects in the room, should be marked with self-luminous colours. Still better is the distribution of a number of weak electric lamps in the room, such as are now used for ornamentation. Even weak mediums can bear faint lights of a phosphorescent character, while stronger light (perhaps by its relation to electrical induction) has a disturbing effect.

All other investigations must and can be undertaken with subdued or bright light, then, what with the visibility of the medium's whole person and visitation and change of clothes before and after the sitting, there will be sufficient control to make sure against conjuring tricks. Altogether to be rejected is every binding of the medium, as a direct challenge to intentional and unintentional deception, and because conjurers in the loosing and retying of knots, and in slipping out and in of loops and fastenings are incredibly expert, so that only a conjurer can be competent to judge of the sufficiency of the fastenings. Besides which, fastening is a kind of supposed security which is painful to the medium, and, therefore, is unworthy, and almost every medium seeks to get free from the bonds as soon as he has fallen into the hypnotic or somnambulic state, and knows himself to be safe from the eyes of the spectators. Whoever relies on bonds, and neglects other control, may always be sure that he is deceived, and all reports of sittings of this kind are at once to be rejected as worthless.

Whoever holds his five senses to be insufficient, with the precautions supposed, to distinguish conjuring from involuntary phenomena, thereby declares the human organs of sense to be unadapted for the establishment of facts generally, and must equally renounce every judicial proof by witnesses and every scientific research. If a skilled conjurer can be introduced as a fourth at every sitting, that is certainly to be recommended, such an one having a professional interest to expose any conjuring, so that mediums may not compromise the vocation of the conjurer. It is notorious that the two best conjurers of Germany and France, Bellachini and Houdin, have given their testimony in favour of the mediums observed by them: other conjurers, on the other hand (Hermann for instance), have asserted their ability to reproduce artificially the same phenomena as those of mediums.

Examining the latter assertions more closely, and running through the anonymous " Confessions of a Medium," Cumberland's " Visitor from the Beyond." or similar revelations, it is at once seen that conjuring requires conditions and presuppositions which are not allowed to the medium. For example, for the writing at a distance one has only to take care that the medium gets the slate in his hand either not at all,or only at the last moment,to prevent a previous preparation, and need only make sure of the hand-holding, or of the secure closure of the slate, to make a direct writing by the finger of the medium impossible. As innumerable reports speak of an audible writing inside well fastened slates held by third persons or lying free upon the table; while some observers assert that they have seen the writing movement of the fragment of pencil on the slate held half under the table, and others even that they have perceived a self-erected pencil writing on paper;* it being also asserted that the writing is suspended when the chain of hands is broken, and is resumed when it is rejoined ; further, that words or sentences, dictated for the first time by one of the circle to the medium after the slate has been fastened up or while the writing is proceeding, have been written within the securely closed slate ; and also that in this way intelligent answers in the closed slate are obtained to written questions unknown to the medium (*Ps. St.* xi. 552); the like phenomena being proved by hundreds of observers, not only with Slade, but also with Monk, Eglinton, and different private mediums : now we may, indeed, doubt the credibility of all these witnesses, but certainly not doubt because under *essentially different* conditions similar

---

* *Psychische Studien*, IV., pp. 468, 545. Owen, " Das Streitige Land," (" The Debateable Land ") translated by Wittig, I., 139.

effects can be attained by conjuring. However, the perusal of such exposures is to be recommended to every one taking part in these experiments, so that he may assure himself against the kinds of deception described.*

As with conjuring, so with the so-called " exposures " of supposed spirit forms ; it is only by a misunderstanding that both are adduced against the facts alleged by so many witnesses. When a supposed apparition is seized, and only the medium is disclosed, an " exposure " has happened for those who imagined that the "apparition" was something else than the medium. But he who has already said that this result is in such cases the probable one, because scarcely five per cent. of the so-called "apparitions" are completely freed (*abgelöst*) from the medium, can no longer speak of " exposure " when the predicted result occurs. He who, rightly or wrongly, expects a phenomenon A, and obtains a phenomenon B, must as an exact investigator first of all examine B, and not play the bully (*pochen*) because B is not A, and in scorn of this result ignore B. He who in such cases is content to laugh at the medium, awakened by a rude shock from his somnambulic state, and not yet master of his senses, instead of immediately passing to the inquiry by what means the before inspected medium has brought about the altered aspect of the "apparition," shows by this conduct that he has no more interest in genuine investigation than have the believers in spirits, but has something quite different in view. Reading the narratives (naturally loosely reported by the newspapers) of "exposures," we soon perceive that the "exposers" have usually shown themselves still less qualified than the believers for experimentation, and are scarcely surprised that every such "exposure" has given a strong impetus to Spiritism.

Conscious and intentional deceptions by the medium can be guarded against, and their unconscious deceptions are among the subjects for investigation. So that it is not be cause a professional medium is to be regarded as a person more or less addicted to deception, that we need be so cowardly as to abjure all research with one, though it is also quite right that private mediums should be preferred. It is a logical fallacy to infer from the fact that a medium has cheated in one case, under certain conditions, that he has been always merely cheating under most different conditions; the conditions of every case have to be examined and one indubitable instance cannot be neutralised by a hundred negative ones. Now since private individuals have neither the requisite circumspection and practice in experimentation, nor the requisite authority with the public, it is most necessary that physicists, physiologists, and psychiatrics of distinction and official position, assisted by conjurers, should be commissioned to enter on this phenomenal province, and to institute long series of experiments with different mediums.

The public has by this time the right to know how the matter stands, and, not being itself in a position to form a judgment, it is dependent on the judgment of the office-bearers of science. The latter refuse to burn their fingers with these things, either because, in their conviction of the infallibility of science up to the present, they consider themselves qualified to decree à *priori* what is possible and what impossible, or merely because they have no desire to exchange the special departments of research with which they are familiar for another. Therefore the Governments must step in, and provide means for research in this department, since it is not to be expected of individuals that they should defray the cost of long series of sittings. Every

---

* Certainly the best of them are the anonymous " Confessions of a Medium " (by Chapman. London : Griffith and Farran. 1882.), whereas Cumberland's " Besucher aus dem Jenseits (" Visitor from the Other Side") Breslau: Schottlander, 1884), is a poor and repulsively affected imitation of the former. There is a German extract from the " Confessions " in Fritz Schultze's " Die Grundgedanken des Spiritismus " ("The Fundamental Ideas of Spiritism.") Leipzig : Gunther, 1885. When a former medium takes to Anti-Spiritism, it follows that he denies his possibly former mediumistic power, and explains all his effects as mere conjuring

prudent man must decline, as Baron Hellenbach did in his time, to deliver a confident judgment on the phenomena until he has had at least a hundred sittings with different mediums ; but that could only be done by rich people with leisure, whose judgment, after sacrifice of their money and time, would have weight for no one but themselves. The existing materials are decidedly insufficient to pronounce the question ripe for *sentence*, but they are quite sufficient to pronounce it one *demanding investigation*. It is the duty of every Government to arrest needless mental confusion and excitement among its citizens, if that can be obviated by means so simple as the appointment of a scientific commission.

Spiritism is at present threatening to become a public calamity, to which every Government has to direct its attention ; but it is not to be eradicated by prohibiting public discussion, as has been attempted in Russia. The superstitious belief in spirits is spreading epidemically, and opens to impostors new ways and means for the exploitation of credulity. All forms of mediæval superstition which were believed to be dead are awaking from their graves, and threaten a renewal of their mischief. These proceedings are already exciting anxiety in the guardians of religion ; the representatives of a finer morality see their efforts overgrown by the re-inforced transcendent Egoism of a sensuously coarse form of belief in immortality. The champions of enlightenment know not what other position to take towards these aberrations than roundly to deny the facts underlying them, and to declare them to be mere fraud and swindling ; from which nothing results but that their honesty is called in question by the Spiritists, and that the belief is screwed up to the point of fanaticism by à *priori* contradiction. In fact, it is doubtful on which side is to be found most superficiality, want of discernment, prejudice, credulity, and incapacity for distinguishing between observed facts and attendant suppositions whether among the Spiritists, who in every accidental fall of an umbrella see the manifestation of a spirit hand, or among the enlighteners, who declare everything to be impossible which does not fit into their narrow picture of the world. It is high time that an end should be put to this state of confusion by official scientific investigation of the phenomena in question, so that the nature of the forces manifested in them should at length be made intelligible, and cease to be conducive to the grossest superstitions.

Having never been myself at a sitting, I am not in a position to form a judgment on the reality of the phenomena ; this much only can I say, that were everything reported true, certainly new forces, hitherto uninvestigated, in man must be admitted, but that this notwithstanding there can be no sort of talk of an overthrow of laws of nature, or of an abandonment of the sphere of the natural. If, for example, a medium rises to the ceiling in a recumbent attitude, that does not prove for me that the law of gravity has been supernaturally suspended in him, but that he must be charged with some force whose repulsion to the earth is stronger than the attraction of gravitation ; just as this is the case with the small elder-pitch figures under the electric clock. He only, therefore, who claims knowledge of the whole range of natural forces, can have the audacity to determine what is possible or impossible, before experience and observation ; but such a claim implying a complete misconception of the limitations of our knowledge, these apodictic predictions only disgrace the judgment of the men of science who allow themselves to be so far carried away.

I have personal knowledge of only two of those who have rendered service in this department of research, Zöllner and Hellenbach. Zöllner's experiments are excellently contrived, give the best conceivable security against conjuring, show everywhere the skilled hand of an accomplished experimenter, and are reported with clearness and precision. It is to be regretted that Zöllner was intent on the confirmation of his hypothesis of a fourth dimension of real space, yet this cannot prejudice the value of the actual results obtained. But unfortunately Zöllner's reports are buried in such a wilderness of polemic, and the four volumes of his "Scientific Treatises" show in the flood of ideas so much that borders on confusion, that in his later years he can no longer be esteemed a classical witness.

Baron Hellenbach is not combative, but a prompt and self-possessed man of the world (*ein schlagfertiger geistesgegenwärtiger Weltmann*) who might well be trusted to see through even astute conjuring; one, moreover, who is penetrated with a sense of the characteristic unreliability of mediums and of the worthlessness of their revelations. On the other hand, his relation to the phenomena and their significance is as little indifferent as Zöllner's; for as with the latter's fourth dimension, so he seeks in them confirmation for his metaphysical standpoint of the transcendental individuality. But what is worse, he holds it unfair (*nicht für loyal*) to make more use of his five senses for taking cognizance of the phenomena than the mediums or apparitions demand or permit. Now I grant that it is unfair (*illoyal*) to roughly clutch hold of a medium or apparition, because an alarming wakening from the somnambulic state may have injurious consequences; but I do not admit that it is unfair to supplement impressions of sight and hearing by judicious contact or by smell. I maintain rather that it is the duty of an investigator not to neglect these additional means when the apparition of a head is four or five inches in front of his own face. For either the apparition is grasped through, or a definitely constituted body, solid or fluid to the hand, is touched; in none of these cases can any harm happen to the medium. As Hellenbach does not recognise this duty, he has, in my view, admitted too favourable chances for deception to be accounted a classical witness. True, Hellenbach's reports of sittings are among the clearest and most precise we possess after those of Zöllner; but if they stood alone I should not feel sustained by them in a demand upon the Government for the appointment of a commission of investigation. But nothing is further from the fact than that their reports stand alone. As regards the physical phenomena, they are best supplemented by the reports of Crookes and Cox, of whom the former, in his experiments with Home, first attempted to provide an exact foundation for the whole province; and the latter, in his work on psychic force, has furnished the best comprehensive report of the department of physical phenomena. Unfortunately Cox, in his observations and disquisitions, has not gone beyond this province, and Crookes, in his experiments in it with Miss Cook, has not observed that degree of critical circumspection which was to be expected of a scientific investigator, since he believed the medium to be secured by an inadequate galvanic fastening,* did not distinguish between detached forms and transfigurations, and did not take into consideration the influence of implanted hallucinations in the production of an illusory transfiguration. However, the report of the four named men are among the most instructive on the subject, and any one wishing to be informed in it cannot do better than begin with the accounts referred to.† It is to

---

* Fastening by grasping the polar extremities, as applied by Crookes and Varley in the physical sittings with Mrs. Fay (*Psychische Studien* II., p. 349-358) may be considered sufficient, but not fastening to the arms with gum, as possible introduction of coins and damp blotting paper allowing the medium to come forward. (*Psychische Studien*, I., p. 341-349.)

† Zöllner's "Wissenschaftliche Abhandlungen" ("Scientific Treatises"). Leipzig: L. Staackmann, 1876-1879, Vol. I., pp. 725-729; Vol. II., Treatise 1, pp. 214, 215, 314, 350; Treatise 2, pp. 909-939, 1173-1180; Vol. III., pp. 231-283. [These passages will be found in the translation entitled "Transcendental Physics."—TR.] Lazar B. Hellenbach's "Mr. Slade's Aufenthalt in Wien" ("Residence in Vienna"). Vienna: J. C. Fischer & Co., 1878; 44 pages. By the same, "Die Vorurtheile der Menschheit" ("The Prejudices of Mankind"), three vols. Vienna: L. Rosner, 1881; pp. 219-255 By the same, "Die neueste Kundgebungen einer intelligiblen Welt" ("The Latest Manifestations of an Intelligible World"). Vienna: L. Rosner, 1880; 68 pages. By the same, "Geburt und Tod als Wechsel der Anschauungsformen oder die Doppelnatur des Menschen" ("Birth and Death as Change of Perceptional Modes, or, the Double Nature of Man") Vienna: W. Branmüller, 1885; pp. 109-115. Crookes' "Spiritualism and Science." Serjeant Cox's "The Theory and Facts of Psychic Force." *Psychische Studien*, Vol. X. (yearly), pp. 120-129, 312-318, 362-371. [References to German editions of English books omitted, as unnecessary for the English reader.—TR.]

be observed that Cox is against the spirit hypothesis, that Crookes and Zöllner have declared neither for nor against it,*but have expressly limited themselves to the study of the phenomena, and that Hellenbach at least thinks very slightingly of the spirit rabble which is so foolish as to occupy itself with us.

The circumstance, which gives to the reports of these men a weight that standing alone they would not possess, is that in the last forty years numberless witnesses have made and published similar and surpassing observations, and that this phenomenal province is as old as the history of mankind. In China and India, among the Siberian Shamans, and the Malayan magicians, among the mystics of the Alexandrian School and in the primitive history of Christianity, in the trials for canonisation of Catholic saints and in the history of the witch-trials, among the alchemists and astrologers of the middle ages, and the vagrant thaumaturgists of the last century,—everywhere there is a recurrence of definite typical forms of abnormal powers and performances.† According to the ideas of the time and the situation of the mediums, they were variously ascribed to gods, nature-spirits, elementary spirits, or demons, to the power of the Holy Ghost or of the Devil, to ancestral spirits, and to a combination of nature spirits and ancestal spirits. The present Spiritism is nothing but the

---

* [I know for a fact that Serjeant Cox became a convert to the spirit hypothesis towards the end of his life. As regards Mr. Crookes, the statement in the text is accurate : but several passages could be quoted from Zöllner (" Transcendental Physics "), showing beyond any doubt that he accepted the agency of invisible intelligences.—Tr.]

† Conf. Hellenbach : "Aus dem Tagebuch eines Philosophen." (" From the Diary of a Philosopher "), IV. " Die mystischen Naturen der Vergangenheit " (" The Mystical Natures of the Past "). Also Jacolliot : " Le Spiritismo dans le Monde. L'initiation et les sciences occultes dans l'Inde " (Paris, 1875). Perty : "Die Mystischen Erscheinungen der menschilchen Natur" ("The Mystical Phenomena of Human Nature"),two vols.(Leipzig and Heidelberg. Wonter,1872.) Schindler : " Das magische Geistesleben " (" The Magical Spirit-Life ") (Breslau, Korn, 1857); and "Der Aberglaube des Mithlatters" ("The Superstition of the Middle Ages "), 1858.

re-appearance and revival of a phenomenal region known to all peoples and in all times, and which has been authoritatively and vehemently denied in the Aufklärung* period.; the spiritistic explanation of the phenomena agrees with that of the Chinese and Indian ancestor-worship, dropping the nature-spirits and diablerie, which are no longer proper to our time.

The Aufklärung period had no respect whatever for facts; it put the world on the head (*stellte die Welt auf den Kopf*), that is, from the rationality of the Aufklärung it decided *à priori* what should and might be, and what not. At present this shallow rationalistic mode of thinking is in conflict with the re-awakened regard for reality, from which weak human reason has first to learn what is possible. The phenomena on which Spiritism founds itself have, therefore, a double interest; first, physically and psychologically, because they widen and complete our knowledge of what is actual, and therefore also possible; and second, historically, because they give us the key to the understanding, in the review of culture, of all superstition and belief in miracle, and of the natural origination of their types in conformity with law. Up to the present, modern historical research is confronted by necromancy, the flight of miracle men, saints, and witches, and by numberless other traditions of the past as by insoluble enigmas; and the hope of finding a satisfactory solution of them must of itself stimulate zeal for research in this department of phenomena, even did that not promise besides the most important elucidations of uninvestigated forces of nature and influences of one mind on another. But everything depends on this research being placed in professional hands, and, before all things, on its not being left exclusively in the hands of those who are guided by no sort of scientific

---

* [The word "enlightenment" expresses a favourable judgment, whereas the German "Aufklärung" has come to be rather descriptive and critical, denoting certain tendencies of an epoch of culture rather than an assumption that its pretensions are well founded. That will be apparent from the context.—TR].

interest, but only by an interest of the heart in verifying the reality of spirits.

In dealing with mediums undoubtedly·one has to do with abnormal natures and phenomena, and it must be recognised that the development and employment of them are injurious to their bodily and mental health. Were the phenomena sufficiently investigated by professional authorities, this circumstance must be enough to dissuade from useless repetitions of such experiments. But as yet this province has been so little examined and elucidated that the theoretical advantage of exploring it seems greater than the injury which may result to individuals. It is, moreover, to be considered that in professional (*berufenen*) hands mediums will be far better taken care of than by dilettantes, because an understanding of the injurious influence of sittings leads to the humane forbearance and medical control, which up to this time mediums have not enjoyed. The phenomena with powerful mediums would be extraordinarily strengthened if they could be got to sit, not daily, but only once or twice a week ; they would also keep their power longer, and their health would be much less prejudiced, perhaps not more than a good constitution could repair by nourishment. As on principle I reprobate all public exhibitions of this sort as a mischief not to be suffered (*Unfug*), so am I equally opposed to the artificial search for mediums by private circles ; I consider it sufficient to develop those mediums whose conspicuous aptitudes are spontaneously manifested. If the Government directed all authorities, magistrates, clergymen, and physicians, on every local occurrence of ghostly knockings, noises, ringing, and stone-throwing, forthwith to hunt up the unconscious medium and to send in reports, in a few years there would be sufficient material of mediums at disposal.

For a rapid survey of this province, W. Schneider's careful synopsis in his book, "The New Spirit Belief"(Der neuere Geisterglaube" : Paderborn. Schönung, 1882), may be recommended, although the entirely mediæval demonology of the Catholic author disregards the fact that the saints and holiest sons and daughters of the Church have displayed exactly the same phenomena as the witches, conjurers, and Spiritists who are presumably assisted by Satan. That the Spiritists, on account of their wicked disposition, must be actually even now punished and rooted out by the Church, as once the magicians and witches, is the good Catholic, if unexpressed, conclusion of this book of 430 pages. For a more thorough acquaintance with the subject I recommend the monthly publication, *Psychische Studien*, a repository of everything worth knowing in the latest phase of Spiritism. In it are to be found all the more important accounts by Zöllner and Hellenbach, as also Cox's work on Psychic Force ; so that, with exception of the first foundation laid by Crookes' experiments, this periodical combines all the necessary material of fact with discussion of the different hypotheses.

The contribution of German philosophy, *pro* and *con.*, has been hitherto very defective. Besides the already cited works of Hellenbach, are first to be mentioned three theistic philosophers, now deceased—J. H. Fichte, Ulrici, and Franz Hoffmann, who went over with song and trumpet (*mit Sang und Klang*) into the Spiritist camp, to avail themselves of the supposed Spiritist proofs of the immortality of the soul. Wundt has published a small anti-spiritist pamphlet, which does not at all enter into the discussion of the matter itself, but pronounces an *à priori* sentence on the problems from the standpoint of the *Aufklärung* From that of Darwinism, Franz Schultze, relying on "The Confession a Medium," and on the above-mentioned book of Schneider, has condemned the whole thing in his work, "The Fundamental Ideas of Spiritism and the Critique of them" ("Die Grundgedanken des Spiritismus und die Kritik derselben" :" Leipzig, Gunther, 1883). Of its three essays only the first treats of modern Spiritism (pp. 3-130), and in this again only the seventh section, giving a bare extract from the "Confessions of a Medium," is noticeable, while the critique of Zöllner's reports in the eighth section is inadequate and superficial.

Among the most circumspect was the deceased disciple of Schopenhauer, Julius Frauenstadt, in his critique of Wallace's "Scientific Aspects of the Supernatural," in the Sunday Supplement of the *Voss. Zgt.*, 1874, No.41 *et seq.*, Noticeable as pointing out the close relations between the older experiments and hypotheses of Reichenbach and the mediumistic phenomena is also the brochure of Leeser : "Herr Professor Wundt und der Spiritismus," 2nd Edition, Leipzig, 1879.

I am, as I have said, not in a position to pronounce upon the reality of unusual phenomena, but I consider the existing testimonies, historical and contemporary, taken in their connection, to be suficient warrant for accepting the existence in the human organism of more forces and capacities than exact science has hitherto investigated and fathomed, and to be an adequately urgent challenge to science to enter upon the exact research of this phenomenal province. On the other hand, I hold myself at any rate competent to offer a conditional judgment on the conclusions to be drawn from these phenomena in case of their reality, for this is peculiarly the office of the philosopher, while he must leave it to the exact sciences to afford the material of fact for his conclusions and inductions. In this region, where certain hallucinations seem for the medium to be almost the indispensable condition of the occurrence of certain phenomena, and the spectators are more or less under the magnetic influence of the medium, and subject to the infection of his hallucinations, I believe it to be psychologically inevitable that judgment should be to some extent prejudiced by frequent participation in mediumistic sittings ; that for the investigator, subjected by them to the power of the mediums and their hallucinations, it must be very difficult, but for the mediums them-

selves almost impossible, to keep the theoretical conclusions
to be drawn from the phenomena independent of the
falsifying impression of the hallucinations experienced, and
that therefore, as regards the eventual consequences of the
phenomena in question, a thinker conditionally judging
from his study is more likely to be free from bias.
Philosophy is, on the whole, right to postpone conclusions
till the material of exact fact is before it in a form tolerably
free from doubt and uncontested ; but when the representatives of exact science hesitate to undertake research in a
particular province of phenomena because they are scared
by inferences almost universally regarded as unavoidable by
both friends and opponents of the subject, a service to the
progress of knowledge may be rendered by the philosophical
critic who dispels these obstructive prejudices, and thereby
first opens the path to unembarrassed scientific investigation. As soon as representatives of exact science are
assured that the *nimbus* of the supernatural, which
superstition has woven about this province, is for criticism
gratuitous prejudice, nothing will remain to prevent the
examination of it. But with the scientific examination
and natural explanation of phenomena supporting belief in
miracle and superstition, they must necessarily lose the
power of nourishing and fortifying such belief and superstition, which the *Aufklärung* has only violently and
externally repressed, but has not inwardly overcome.

It would be wearisome to repeat, whenever a phenomenon
is referred to, the reservation that any explanation is only
conditional on the reality of the fact, and that for this
reality I neither can nor will in the least vouch. I therefore beg that this protestation, here once for all expressed,
may in what follows be throughout remembered. I must
also observe that it would be impossible within the narrow
limits of a pamphlet to make the reader exactly acquainted
with the phenomena in question, for which an extensive
volume would be requisite. I must, from regard to space,

confine myself to founding discussion upon some typical
form of the phenomena, and as for the rest refer to the
sources.

II.

THE PHYSICAL PHENOMENA.

If different persons are tested in respect to the control
of their conscious wills over their involuntary muscles, very
different results are obtained. No one is able wholly· to
suppress all involuntary muscular movements for more than
a few minutes together ; with normal persons, however,
these involuntary movements fluctuate about a mean prescribed by the conscious will, not diverging far or long from
that. With a minority of persons it is otherwise ; the deviations become more considerable with time, leading at
length to combined movements, very important in degree
and very different in kind. If, for example, a string ·with
weight attached is held with outstretched arm over a scale,
in the case of abnormal natures, there will soon be considerable involuntary deviations of the weight from the spot
fixed upon. Physiology teaches that such involuntary
muscular movements do not proceed from those parts of the
cortices of the large brain in which conscious will has its
seat, but from middle parts of the brain ; that with normal
natures the reflex-inhibiting power of the large brain
suffices to restrain such movements within practically insig-
nificant limits, but that with abnormal natures the relative
independence of the middle brain parts upon the supporter
of the conscious will can attain a considerable degree.

Since the activity of these middle brain parts has
usually only a preparatory or executive value, and, therefore, as a rule, for the human self-consciousne s remains

unconscious, we have here to do with a relatively unconscious activity of the brain, the results of which are expressed by involuntary muscular movements. In so far also as memory, intelligence, and desires accede to these middle brain parts, the results of the involuntary muscular activity produced by the latter might very well appear to emanate from an intelligent and characterised personality, notwithstanding that the waking self-consciousness of the person performing these movements knew nothing of its unconscious brain activity causing the same. Nay, such person need not even be sensible of his involuntary muscular activity, and may thus, with a good conscience, deny his mental origination and bodily mediation of the phenomena occurring, while yet he is the sole cause of them. This theory of involuntary muscular activity and unconscious brain activity was first started and expounded by the English physiologist Carpenter, * and may now be considered as fairly recognised. Carpenter has only committed the mistake of holding his theory to be an exhaustive explanation of all mediumistic phenomena, and of discreditably (*in illoyaler Weise*) attacking the investigators who, like Crookes, dispute this pretension.

If several persons sit in the dark, in tense expectation, with hands on a table, frequently one or other of them is an abnormal nature, in the sense that after some time he developes involuntary muscular action, and moves the table, although he can swear that he has not willed to move it, and has detected no involuntary motion of his arms and hands. To find out who the person is, it is only necessary to address the table, proposing that it should signify " no " by one rap," doubtful" by two, and "yes " by three raps. If the table agrees by three raps, it is next to be asked whether A, or B, or C, is the medium, till instead of the negative one gets the affirmative reply by the raps. It should then further

* The author's references are to *Psychische Studien ;* but the English reader may be referred to the original work, " Mental Physiology."—TR.

be asked whether the arrangement of the circle is favourable for phenomena, or should be altered in order to free the medium from disturbing influences, or if any one should be excluded as a disturbing element. In the answers are reflected the unconscious antipathies and sympathies of the medium towards the rest of the party, and after obedience to these indications the phenomena will become much more distinct. One can then proceed to get the alphabet rapped off, the numeral order of a letter in the alphabet being signified by the number of raps, and thus, by a very detailed process, it is true, carry on conversation with the unconsiously functioning brain of the medium.

The conversation is expedited by application of involuntary arm or hand movements to the designation of the letters, as by suspending a weight attached to a string over an alphabet,* or of involuntary pressure of the hand upon a pointer revolving upon an alphabetical plate, or upon the latter revolving under a stationary pointer. In each case the unconsciously functioning parts of the medium's brain must be first used to the conditions, many mistakes with the letters, requiring great patience for rectification, being made before this practice is acquired.

Still quicker than with such so-called " psychographs" or " Spiritoscopes" is the conversation when the medium writes directly with pen or pencil. This involuntary writing is abundantly proved in the case of the insane; when it occurs with the sane they are called "writing mediums." They can often only get the involuntary writing with the left hand, and then it is usually reversed (*Spiegelschrift*). Many involuntary writers reverse even with the right hand. With most the involuntary handwriting differs in character from their ordinary writing, and often resembles

---

* Entirely similar to the motions of such a string, is, in its origin, the motion of the divining rod, only that the latter is not used to point out le'tters, but for manifestation of sensitive impressions of the lower nerve ce ntres, especially of the obscure feelings excited in sensitives by the proximity of water or metals. The problem of the divining rod, which plays so important a part in well-seeking and treasure-digging, is already solved in principle (*end gultig*) by Reichenbach in his work, " Sensitive Man" ("Der sensitive Mensch.").

that of those from whom the communication purports to come. Involuntary writing often occurs in full consciousness, in the middle of a cheerful conversation, and apparently as mechanically and heedlessly as an idle play of the fingers. For conversation it is less adapted than raps or the psychograph, because it prefers to follow its own caprices and dreamy courses, and allows the widest facility for intentional deceptions.

With involuntary writing is here to be mentioned involuntary speaking, which however usually occurs in waking unconsciousness, thus in a state of convulsion or ecstacy (trance). In this way are recited speeches and poems, learnt by rote, as also independent lectures and sermons, mostly on religious or other ideal subjects of emotional interest. The "speaking with tongues" of the early Christian communities is only to be understood as involuntary speech in a religiously motived ecstacy. Here the muscles of speech, as in writing those of the hand, are innerved by involuntary brain activity of the middle central organs, and as with the change of handwriting, so here the voice takes an altered ring and intonation, resembling that of a particular person, if the medium has the illusion that this person is speaking through him.

In the case of speaking mediums, it is quite clear that one has to do with a somnambulic state,* conditioned by psychical excitement ; with writing mediums an externally insensitive trance-condition without waking consciousness can exist during the writing, yet the waking consciousness can persist apparently undisturbed, engaging in cheerful discourse, while the unconscious activity of the middle parts of the brain simultaneously effects the involuntary writing. Now there are here two possible cases ; either the unconscious brain activity in question is an absolutely unconscious, purely material process, following prescribed mechanical paths, and only presenting in its results the semblance of

---

* Compare my essay ; "Somnambulism" ("Moderne Probleme". W. Friedrich, Leipzig, 1885.)

28

conscious intelligence, in consequence of the mechanical
paths pursued having been formerly levelled and prescribed
by relatively conscious psychical activity, or with and
behind the waking consciousness there is a somnambulic
consciousness accompanying these mechanical material brain
processes and enlightening them with real intelligence.

If the involuntary writing only repeated what had been
learnt by rote, or put together fragments of memory in an
accidental unintelligent manner, the first side of the
alternative would be sufficient, and as the simpler would be
preferable. But as in these productions the government
of a productive phantasy and of a regulating intelligence
is, up to a certain degree, unmistakable, the decision must
be for the co-existence of two consciousnesses in different
parts of the brain. This phenomenon must therefore be
called somnambulism, but somnambulism masked, that is
veiled and made unrecognisable for external observation, by
the persistence of the waking consciousness. This masked
somnambulism is to be considered as a transition state
between the single dominion of the waking consciousness
and that of the somnambulic consciousness, and can pass
through the most different degrees as regards the relative
clearness of the two consciousnesses; these steps leading
successively from the first emergence of the somnambulic
consciousness above the threshold, when the waking consciousness is still apparently unchanged, through half-
dreamy states of impaired circumspection and accountability
(as in second sight), up to complete extinction of the
sensibility of the waking consciousness.*

What till now, with Carpenter, we have called unconscious cerebration, we could thus just as well name the

* This masked somnambulism plays a part in seers and mystics not yet
sufficiently observed and examined. As the effectiveness (*virtuosität*) of
second-sight or mystic intuition developes, the necessity there at first was,
that the normal consciousness should be extinguished to make way for the
ecstatic condition, diminishes; and from a certain degree of effectiveness onwards, the seer and mystic can so command the ecstatic vision that it
co-exists and is interchangeable with normal consciousness. With Andrew
Jackson Davis, for example, the periods of open and masked somnambulism can
be traced as successive sections of his life.

activity of somnambulic consciousness, and assert that the involuntary muscular movements of mediums, in so far as by their results they discover a co-operating intelligence, are occasioned and guided by activity of somnambulic consciousness, whether this latter, by extinction of the waking consciousness, is apparent to by-standers, or whether it is masked by the persistence of the waking consciousness. By a medium we shall have to understand an individual who either casually or by self-induced psychical excitation. falls spontaneously into manifest or masked somnambulism. Mediums are usually in manifest somnambulism : first, in the involuntary speaking; secondly, at the production of physical phenomena requiring an extraordinary exertion of nerve force ; and thirdly, for the implantation of hallucinations in the spectators, for which a special intensity of the hallucinations in the medium himself seems to be a condition precedent. Most of the other phenomena happen in the condition of a masked somnambulism, and it is just this condition which most easily induces deceptions as to the causes of the phenomena, as well in the spectators who are unaquainted with it, as in the medium himself. The understanding of masked somnambulism is, therefore, the key to the whole province of mediumistic phenomena.

It is further characteristic of mediums that they are auto-somnambules; that is,that without the influence of a magnetiser and without mechanical aids, thus by merely psychical aids, they place themselves in masked or manifest somnambulism. It is just this self-disposing to somnambulism when desired which requires considerable practice before it can be commanded with some confidence at the wish of strangers ; it also very easily refuses, the sittings being then failures. The investigations of Fahnestock have shown that every one has the latent capacity for voluntary auto-somnambulism by merely psychical means, and that many persons by practice can come to effect this transition at any time

with tolerable rapidity. They have shown further, that
one can awake from this condition by mere force of will,
but also that this waking can be voluntarily accomplished
with restriction to certain parts of the body (as the head
alone, or the upper part of the body alone, or only the
head and half the body), and even that the whole body,
with exception of a single limb, can be awakened from the
somnambulic state.*

The effect in such cases is that the waking consciousness
resumes its functions and its conscious will resumes control
over the awakened parts of the body, but that the parts
not yet awakened are still withdrawn from that control,
and remain exclusively subject to the somnambulic consciousness, and.in the absence of any impulse from the
somnambulic parts of the brain appear cataleptic. This
remarkable phenomenon of locally confined, or locally
removed, hypnotism is confirmed by the latest French
researches in somnambulism. According to Fahnestock,
practice at length enables the direct withdrawal of particular
parts of the body from the conscious will and sensibility,
and their subjection to a condition in itself cataleptic, but
in fact sensitive and compliant to every innervation-
impulse of the somnambulic consciousness. In this condition, which makes itself known by a fall in the temperature
of the skin in the limb affected, there is no longer any
accord between the innervation-impulses of the somnambulic
parts of the brain and the reflex-inhibitions and voluntary
acts of the waking consciousness, so that the limb in
question is subject alone and exclusively to the somnambulic
impulses.

This condition of local catalepsy for waking consciousness can the more easily occur, when there is besides a
general condition of masked somnambulism, with which

* "Statuvolism, or Artificial Sonambulism" by Wm. Baker Fahnestock, M.D·
(German translation by Dr. Wittig) *Psych. Stud.*, X. pp. 115-120, 169-173, 204
(Published in America, but can be procured through the Psychological Press,
16, Craven-street, Charing Cross S.W.—TR.)

Fahnestock is unacquainted; such local catalepsy and insensibility must, however, completely deceive the medium himself into the belief that the acts performed by him with this limb, by reason of the somnambulic innervation-impulse, are not his at all. It is a constantly recurring observation, that the hand of a medium, which by means of still uninvestigated nerve forces produces extraordinary phenomena (as writing at a distance without contact with the pencil), is cold, it being a rule that the fall of temperature immediately precedes the phenomena (*Ps.St.* XI. 498.)* In some very extraordinary phenomena, *e.g.*, the penetration of the medium's arm by an iron ring, it is reported that the medium's hands become as cold as those of a corpse laid upon ice. (*Ps. St.* III. 55.)

Here, however, the passing of a limb into the cataleptic or hypnotic state is to be regarded as a phenomenon not conditioned by the will, but involuntarily brought about, with reference to the aim of the somnambulic consciousness. Waking consciousness and its conscious will only give, first, the impulse to the medium to place himself in masked or manifest somnambulism, and secondly the general directive, what sort of phenomenon is wished for and expected ; the somnambulic consciousness set going may take cognizance of these wishes and directions up to a certain point, often, however, not at all, and even when it has regard to them, the result is usually somewhat different from that expected, generally falling short of the latter, but sometimes exceeding it. How the somnambulic consciousness of the medium begins to carry into execution the design, which with or without regard to the wishes of the waking consciousness it sets, that is, how it obtains mastery over the involuntary muscular activity and the still uninvestigated

---

* [In confirmation the translator may refer to his own report in " LIGHT, April 19th, 1884. " We (Mr. Roden Noel and myself) noticed two facts (always observed likewise with Slade), one of which, certainly, could not result from any voluntary act of the medium. This was the lowering of the temperature of the hand which held the slate just before and after the writing. The other fact was the cessation of the sound of writing when Mr. Eglinton broke the contact of his hand with my own."—TR.]

forces of the organism, we as yet know just as little, as how the conscious will begins to obtain mastery over the voluntary muscular movements and animal magnetism. It is certain that here also practice has great influence, but again that with wholly inexperienced mediums the most astonishing phenomena can involuntarily occur, of the connection of which with themselves the mediums have no suspicion whatever.

An universal medium must be more than an auto-somnambule ; he must be at the same time a powerful magnetiser. There are strong magnetisers who have no tendency to somnambulism, and such are not to be called mediums, because their somnambulic consciousness is never so far liberated from their conscious wills as to arrive at the production of mediumistic results. Their operations are limited to magnetising other persons, either locally or totally, and in the latter case making somnambules of them ; but it is a question whether the conscious will may not be trained to direct its magnetic force to other than living objects, and thus succeed in the conscious voluntary production of some at least of the mediumistic phenomena. There is here, of course, no question of the involuntary muscular effects hitherto occupying us, but of another province of physical phenomena, the experimental conditions of which must be so arranged as indubitably to exclude the co-operation of involuntary muscular action.

As the basic phenomenon of this department I consider the following. Out of two balls of limewood, of about 7cm. diameter, a thin wand of 30cm. length, and a horsehair, Dr. R. Friese, of Breslau, constructed a horizontal torsion balance. If a strong physical medium approaches the tips of the fingers of one hand to one of the two balls, a repulsion, though certainly an excessively slight one, takes place. But if the medium has clasped this ball in his hand a minute before, or only breathed upon it, there is now an attraction between the ball and the hand, much stronger than the previous repulsion, so that the ball can easily be drawn slowly round in a circle. (*Ps. St.* VIII. 381.) This experiment must first be repeated and extended by others, with especial observation of the mutual behaviour of two balls of different torsion balances after being held in the hand. The signification of the experiments can only be, that the medium's hand is charged with a force repellant of the neutral, *i.e.*, uncharged wooden ball, but is in a far higher degree attractive to the charged ball of the same name. This behaviour is reversely analogous to the case of frictional electricity and magnetism.

The relation of the force in question to that of frictional electricity shows itself, among other respects, also in its dependence on the degree of atmospheric moisture, and in the faculty, established by Reichenbach, Fechner,* Zöllner, and many others, which mediums have of violently disturbing the enclosed magnetic needle without contact. A magnetiser possesses the faculty of so charging a person that between him and the metal bedstead, from which he is isolated by a woollen covering, a strong discharge of sparks takes place on accidental approximation of a part of the body; this I have proved in myself after careful investigation of the magnetiser and his surroundings,† and I leave it undecided whether this is a case of explosive equilibriation of the mediumistic nerve force itself, or of a previous conversion of this force into electricity. Electrical crepitation is one of the most ordinary and frequent phenomena at mediumistic sittings. The next investigation must be into the behaviour of the force in question, first to the poles of large, freely-suspended bar magnets, secondly to the electroscope, thirdly to freely suspended wires with galvanic currents, and fourthly to the strength of galvanic currents in

---

* "Erinnerungen an die letzten Tage der Odlehre und ihres Urhebers" ("Recollection of the last days of Od and its author"). Leipzig : Breitkopf and Härtel, 1876. [See " Transcendental Physics," c. 2.]

† "Phil. d. Unb." [The author's "Philosophy of the Unconscious." The English reader will find the passages referred to in Mr. Coupland's translation, of the 9th edition, vol. II., p. 176.—Tr.]

fixed conductors. It is incomprehensible, and of the worst significance for the scientific interests of Spiritists, that no one has yet made even an attempt to approach these questions.

A large number of the mediumistic phenomena are confined to the sliding up of objects to the medium. The repulsion of objects seems also to occur, but is much less frequent. Cox never saw the one, but very often the other, and has described it very graphically. He compares the nature of the motion with that of steel filings attracted by a magnet on a level surface. " They first rise a little, fall down, move forward, pause, till they are within the influence of the magnetic force, when they leap to the magnet (medium) with a sudden spring." (*Ps. St.* X., 127,128.) He saw chairs slide up to the medium in this way from a distance of from six to ten feet, armchairs and sofas advance two to three feet ; he once saw a heavy armchair, fourteen feet away, come up to the medium.* The stronger a medium is, the larger is the sphere of his efficacy, but it is always limited, and the difficulties to be overcome are not proportional to the size, but

---

* Presuming that the author will not object to an additional fact, in two important respects in advance of the above, being here adduced, the translator cites a statement of his own in the *Spiritualist* of November 26th, 1876, repeated by him on oath as a witness in the Slade case, when he was cross-examined upon it by the solicitor for the prosecution. " A chair at my side of the table was flung down.• I produced a tape measure, and took the nearest distance between the medium and the chair, as the latter lay upon the floor ; it was five feet, and I could see a good clear space between the table and the prostrate chair. I requested Slade not to stir, and asked that the chair, which lay on my right, and which I could watch, as Colonel Olcott sat on my other side,might be picked up and placed by me. In a few minutes, during which time the medium never moved, the chair was drawn a few inches towards me, and as I watched it and the open space between it and the table, medium, and everything else, it was suddenly jumped upon its legs and deposited at my side." This was on the 14th October, 1875, in New York, and at Slade's (the medium's) own lodgings. But besides that the room (carpeted) and furniture had been more than once examined by me for attachments, &c. The test here being impromptu, and suggested by myself on the spur of the moment, the genuine character of the phenomenon can hardly be doubted, with the supposition, of course, of my veracity and accuracy. The two circumstances which make the case worth quoting in relation to Dr. v. Hartmann's explanations are (1) that the chair approached me, who am not in the least mediumistic, and was not in a line with Slade (though I was with Colonel Olcott, who may have been a medium),and (2) that besides the force, there was an evident intelligence giving it a new direction and an extraordinary impulse in compliance with my wish. (To this note, as to a former one, I have to add that it will not appear in the reprint, except with Dr. v. Hartmann's authority.)

to the weight of the objects. The question here is, how a medium begins to charge a particular object with his force ; what course does the force take in transmission, and by what means is it conducted? Here also experimental results might be obtained (by isolating the medium from the floor, interposition of different materials between the medium and the object attracted, &c.).

It is clear that there is here no question, either of muscular action, or of immediate mental influence of the medium on the material objects, but only of a physical force produced under psychical excitation by the medium's nervous system. It seems unintelligible, therefore, why Cox should have given to this force the misleading appellation "Psychic" instead of "Nerve" force, since he himself expressly describes it as *physical* (thus not psychical), distinguishing it only from *muscular* force. (*Ps. St.* X., 213, 214.)

An influence surpassing mere repulsion and attraction between medium and objects is manifested by nerve force when it changes the dynamical relation between objects and the earth. As before the torsion balance, so here the scales have to establish the ground phenomenon, Crookes and most other experimenters having made use of the spring balance. It is a question whether for free experiments the scale or lever balance should not be preferred, in order first to ascertain if and in what degree small wooden balls might vary in weight by being charged with mediumistic nerve force. The application, as by Crookes, of a self-registering apparatus to the balances is to be recommended in all experiments, because only the permanent mechanical indication of the apparatus itself secures from the suspicion that the person reading off the record was under the influence of an hallucination implanted in him by the medium. To exclude involuntary muscular action, Crookes placed two vessels of water, one within the other, over the fixed fulcrum of the board, which was suspended at the end by a spring balance, and made the medium dip his hand into the water of the upper, fixed vessel.* Others have attached a table to the torsion balance, the medium or mediums kneeling on revolving stools, with hands at some distance from the table. Cox thus saw the weight of an 8lb. table vary between 5lb. and 85lb., according to wish that it should be heavy or light. (*Ps. St.*, X. 127.) Chambers and Owen saw a table of 121lb. under similar conditions vary to between 60lb. and 144lb.† Of Indian fakirs the following performance is reported : earth is thrown into a flowerpot, and small sticks are set upright in it ; on these are thrust perforated sheets of paper ; after some minutes the sheets begin slowly and tremulously to rise up and down, the fakir standing several feet off. The objects are neither brought nor touched by the fakir. It is a very common phenomenon at mediumistic sittings for the table, with everything on it, to rise of itself, or for a chair with someone on it to be slightly raised, either without contact by the medium, or with his contact in a position and attitude excluding the supposition of muscular action.‡ Somnambules in the bath show sometimes a diminution of their normal weight, sufficing to keep them floating with immersion of but a small part of the body, and the obstinacy with which whole centuries adhered to the water proof of witches suggests that the latter, falling into reflex-hypnotism through fear, sometimes experienced a diminution of weight. On this same reduction of weight in the ecstatic condition rests also the direct proof of weight by the " witch-scales." Lastly, we hear of mediums being raised in the air, sometimes in dark sittings,

---

* Crookes. (A full description of this contrivance and of the experiment, with illustrations, will be found in Crookes' "Researches into the Phenomena of Spiritualism." Burns, 15, Southampton Row. 1874.)

† Owen : "The Debateable Land." *Ps. St.*, II. 113.

‡ [I was sitting once with Slade, in New York, by bright daylight, when his chair was forced back from the table. My own chair being clear from the table, so that I commanded a full view of Slade's legs and feet, I asked that the chair on which I was sitting might also be pushed back with me on it. This was immediately done, two or three inches, the motion being at right angles to the medium.—TR.]

when they write something on the ceiling, sometimes also by subdued gas-light. (*Ps. St.* VI., 566.)
This flying is also reported of Jamblichus, Faust, of various
witches and saints, the testimony being especially strong
in the case of Joseph of Copertinus, pronounced a saint
two years after his death, who is even said twice to have
raised another in the air with him. (*Ps. St.* IV., 241 *et seq.*)
The condition of the levitation seems always to be the completely somnambulic state of the medium; but since this
is likewise most adapted to the transmission of hallucinations to the spectators, and it is usually after a number of
sittings with the same circle—and then at the close of the
sitting, when those present have become susceptible to the
implantation of hallucinations—that this phenomenon
occurs, it is here particularly necessary to confirm its objective
reality by durable proofs.*

The phenomena in question are only explicable by a
polarity of nerve force in analogy with frictional electricity.
Were it a case of repulsion only of charged bodies from
the earth in opposition to gravitation, a simple force would
do ; but as the dynamical relations of bodies charged with
nerve force to the earth are sometimes conformable and
sometimes opposed to gravitation, apparently a double sort
of charging, dependent on the somnambulic will of the
medium, must be admitted. And this is inferable back also
to the attraction and repulsion of objects by the medium, as
his repulsion to all neutral bodies must be the
same. The explanation by a polaric force had been
already advanced by the old Indians, who asserted that
the force of gravity is suppressed and transformed into its
opposite by conversion of the polarity of the body. It may
here be remembered that Zöllner has attempted to explain
universal gravitation from the statical effects of electricity,†

---

* It is quite easy to excite in a somnambule the hallucination that the
magnetiser is flying round the room. (*Psych. Stud.* III., 536, 537.) See p. 114.

† Zöllner's " Erklärung der universellen Gravitation aus den statischen
Wirkungen der Electricitat und die allgemeine Bedeutung des Weberschen
Gesetzes." (Leipzig : Staackmann, 1882.) *Cf.* his "Wiss Abh.," p 1, No. 3.

and that with all difference of different natural forces they are undoubtedly but derivatives from the same primitive forces. If Zöllner's view is granted, and the supposition is made that the nerve force alters the statical-electrical condition of the body, on which its gravitation depends, we should in fact have to do with only one force, which not merely neutralises or outweighs the action of the force of gravity, but augments, reduces, or negatives the force of gravity itself, without it being permissible on that account to speak of a suspension or breach of the laws of nature.

The behaviour of floating objects is similar, according to Cox, to that of a small air balloon; their weight is never changed suddenly, but gradually; they ascend gently and without jerk, coming down in the same way, but always with light pendulous oscillations. No harm has ever been done when tables, with lighted petroleum lamps on them, have risen, the quietness of the motion, and the slowness and slightness of the oscillations not occasioning overthrow of the lamps. Besides the oscillations, the floating objects exhibit tremors, such as may be most clearly seen from the automatic curves of Crookes' experiments, and which are unmistakably connected with the simultaneous pulse-curves of the medium, as the sphygmograph would show them. This is the most distinct proof that the force really proceeds from the medium, and from the medium alone. All mediumistic phonomena are, moreover, not constant, but fluctuate continually in irregular waves, in correspondence with the innervation waves streaming from the medium's middle brain into his organism.

The results usually gain in strength when the medium is not alone, but in a small circle of both sexes. It seems as if a medium has the power of making those present more or less mediums also, that is, of occasioning them unconsciously to develope nerve force, and that he is further able definitely to influence the distribution and application of

the general nerve force thus developed. It takes a period
of from a few minutes to several quarters-of-an-hour
to charge the place and the medium sufficiently for the
production of extraordinary effects. These, therefore,
happen mostly at the close of sittings, or at least in the
latter half of them, and they are more intense the more
mediums—that is, persons developing nerve force—there are
present, by whose unconscious co-operation the principal
medium is supported. For weak mediums, therefore, a
"circle" is strictly indispensable, and only strong mediums
can elicit important effects also alone ; regard should be
had to this in experiments with inexperienced or moder-
ately qualified mediums.

From the combination of the action of attraction and
répulsion with that which alters the weight of objects
already result the most manifold phenomena. The floating
objects can advance to and retreat from the medium through
the air as well as by horizontal motion. The same object
(as a small table) can for instance slide along the floor from
the medium, rise in the remotest corner of the room, and
then hover down or fall obliquely on the séance table.
Water rises unseen from a can standing apart, and descends
in a drizzle on the spectators. It happens again and again
that bells ring in a house at certain hours for days or
weeks together, and go on ringing, or are torn down, notwithstanding all fastening and muffling, * or that premises
are regularly bombarded with stones, coals, or other things
lying about, without the police or those privately posted for
observation being able to discover a trace of the originator
of the mischief.† Usually there turns out to be a servant-
maid, or an hysterical female, or a child in the years of
development, by whose presence in the place the phenomenon
is conditioned, and in whose proximity the projectiles fall.
The officials and private people have seldom any suspicion

---

* Owen : "The Debateable Land."

† Wallace : " Defence of Modern Spiritualism." *Ps. St.* VII., 237, 562 ; VIII.
5, 81-103, 188, 238, 471 ; IX., 6-15, 39-40, 94-96.

of such connection, and rather believe in ghost pranks than that it is a medium unconsciously perpetrating the mischief.

Considering that the different objects in the sitting-room and the different persons present are in different degrees charged, partly through distribution by the medium of the collective force, partly through active co-operation, it is intelligible that the lighter objects, especially when floating, are subject simultaneously to very different attractions and repulsions, and follow the most tortuous paths. If the medium directs, by repulsion, an object to where the attractive sphere of one of the party predominates, the object glides or floats to that person, and to that part of the body, it may be a hand, which is most charged. Thus is to be explained, for instance, Hellenbach's experience of a slate creeping up his body to the hand.

The mediumistic nerve force can further variously combine with involuntary muscular activity, which at sitting round a table is usually the first thing developed, the charging with nerve force gradually increasing till that alone suffices ; so that the objects at first only move by contact, but afterwards without.

Nor do the above phenomena exhaust the effects of mediumistic nerve force. Especially noticeable is its expansive counteraction of the cohesion of material particles, expressed by sudden discharges in the nature of electrical reports. When the explosive discharge, which always occurs in a closely circumscribed spot, and indeed usually in the interior of bodies, does not overcome the material cohesion, it announces itself to the sense of touch as a tremulous concussion, and is perceptible to hearing by a stronger or weaker crackling or rapping sound. When it overcomes cohesion, there is besides a tearing to pieces or shattering of the object. (Zöllner's bed-screen * and tumbler.) The rap sounds begin with the faintest crepitations (as with an

---

* "Transcendental Physics." Translation, c. 2.—TR.

electrical machine), sometimes increasing to uproarious din
and clatter;* they resound sometimes from tables, chairs.
partitions, walls; sometimes from small utensils, sometimes from massive rocks;† and it seems that the louder
can be localised as well by vibrations sensible to touch as
by the ear. Observation by the microtelephone from a graet
distance and registration by the phonograph are always
to be desired, in order to distinguish possibly transferred
hallucinations of hearing and touch from objective
occurrences.

Similar sounds constantly occur in the most different
places, with or without the movement of utensils and furniture, no one in the house or the neighbourhood being in
the least able to trace the cause. As with the stone-
throwing mentioned above, there is always a medium,
usually of the female sex, who is, at first quite unconsciously,
the cause. Should the neighbourhood come to suspect this
causal connection, there is generally a combination of the
brutality of the lower police with the narrow and zealous
superstition of parsondom and populace to drive the poor
nervous patient quite distracted, instead of her being placed
under medical treatment, or of her mediumistic aptitudes
being systematically utilised for experiment.

We encounter a specially improbable class of phenomena
in reports relating to the penetration of matter. The Indian
reporcs regard them as indisputable facts, and explain them
by the dissipation and re-condensation of the elementary
constituents of the material object. A wrought-iron ring
shall get upon the arm of the medium while the latter's
hand or finger is grasped by one of the party; Reimers and
Aksakow have seen the experiment succeed when the hand
of the holder was bound to the medium's arm (*Ps. St.* I.,
544; III., 52-54); and Olcott even asserts that he observed
the side of the ring, applied to the medium's arm, dissolve as
it were into a vapour, thus permitting penetration of the

---

* Owen: "Debateable Land."   † Id.

arm. (*Ps. St.* III., 56.)* Zöllner's observations of similar occurrences are numerous, the passing of coins, slate-pencils, &c., through closed boxes and table surfaces, placing a ring round the leg of a table, tying of knots in sealed strings and strips, and so on ; † and a great part of these phenomena have been repeated by private mediums. (*Ps. St.* VII., 390, 392.) According to Hare, two balls of platinum were conveyed into a sealed glass tube.‡ Even with presupposition of the greatest expertness in untying and retying knots, and in stripping off and on of nooses and fastenings, there remain a multitude of accounts in which the mode of applying and sealing the fastenings, and the inviolableness of the seals after the processes, appear as exclusive of this obvious explanation as is the briefness of the interval available for such manipulations. It is there fore generally accepted among the Spiritists that a medium in the somnambulic state is able, by the penetration of matter, to get free from and to resume every sort of fastening.

The mediumistic stone-throwing, by which window panes, &c., are usually broken, often happens also when the medium is in a closed room, the stones coming from outside, and being visible first in the room when five or six feet from the floor. (*Ps. St.* VIII., 5-12.) Water sprinkling happens, no water having been before in the room, though with Zöllner's experiences of this there was a can of water in the next room. The "apport" of objects from other rooms or houses, or of flowers which were growing in the open air,

---

* Olcott's "People from the Other World." (Hartford, Conn., U.S.A. : American Publishing Company. 1875.) Page 260 (with illustration) : "There was just distance enough between our arms for the large ring to touch both his (medium's) and mine, and at the moment of the shock, it seemed to me that the side of the ring next to Horatio's (medium's) dissolved into a vapour, while the one next to mine remained solid, for it moved away from my skin directly through his arm, or else opened so as to permit his to pass through its own substance, and the next instant it dangled upon my wrist."—TR.

† "Transcendental Physics," *passim:*—TR.

‡ Robert Hare, M.D., Professor of Chemistry at the University of Pennsylvania, and author of many chemical and physical treatises, inventor of the contrivance known in textbooks of physics as "Hare's Spiral," &c. An account of the experiment referred to in the text will be found in "Transcendental Physics," p. 151, *et seq.*—TR.

into the séance room, is one of the commonest of mediumistic phenomena, but the earthly origin of the objects introduced can always be proved. The stones are dry or wet, warm or cold, according to the weather, and marked stones, after being put out of doors, have often fallen a second time in the house. Were these phenomena connected with a fourth dimension of real space, as Zöllner thought, we should expect that material objects not belonging to our three-dimensional world would be introduced ; from the contrary it must be concluded that Zöllner's explanation is not the right one, but that the entire course of the phenomena belongs as much to our three-dimensional world as does the material employed in them. The occasional incalescence, or traces of it, which Zöllner says he observed, likewise points rather to molecular disturbances of material cohesion than to motions and oscillations beyond three-dimensional space, which would not occasion molecular disturbances and changes of temperature.

Also to be noticed are the phenomena of lights, which almostnever wholly fail at sittings with powerful mediums. They are usually so weak as only to be observed in the dark, and even then only by a sensitive sight. Exceptionally, however, they attain greater strength, so that all see them. It seems still questionable whether the appearance of light observed by Zöllner on the wall, and which was broken by the shadows of the feet of the table, really signified a source of light beyond the table, or whether it was not formed direct ; as also it remains in the first case doubtful, whether the parallel beams of light really proceeded from an infinitely remote source, or whether these transverse ether vibrations in parallel directions were not occasioned by wholly different means and in a wholly different way than by illuminating material (light vibrations of particular material particles at a particular place).* Sensitives and somnambules often see luminous phenomena which appear to

* See "Transcendental Physics, c. 12 for Zöllner's account of this phenomenon and his inferences.—TR.

them to come from an infinite distance, but the involuntary conclusion of sense, founded on the ordinary originating causes of ether vibrations, need not correspond with the facts.

For the study of these questions we must decidedly revert to the experiences of Reichenbach, who asserts the odic diaphaneity of many substances which for ordinary rays of light are impenetrable. It seems that we have here in many cases to do with ether vibrations of higher frangibility and of another kind, which are first converted into light vibrations in the eye of the sensitive (or of one made temporarily sensitive by the medium). This is confirmed by experiments of the photographer Beattie, who obtained on the plates different appearances of lights which were invisible to him and his companions, but the photographic forms of which agreed with the descriptions given by mediums, of lights seen by them at different spots during the exposure. (*Ps. St.* V., 339 ; VIII., 257.) These photographic experiments must be extensively followed up, for the safe distinction between what in these luminous phenomena are implanted hallucination, and what objective vibration processes. So far as it is a case of true ether vibrations of high frangibility, we may speculate on forms of conversion of the mediumistic nerve force, analogous to the conversion of electricity into light of high frangibility. On the other hand, these phenomena must first be investigated with complete exactitude, and all attempts at a three-dimensional explanation must be entirely exhausted before approaching one from the hypothetical fourth dimension, as Zöllner, it is evident, too hastily did.

If the mediumistic nerve force can, on the one hand, be converted into phenomena of light and heat, and on the other, has the property of accumulating at limited points in a degree of intensity leading to explosive discharge, it is scarcely surprising if such discharges, like electric sparks, are able to kindle combustible substances, for instance, the new wick of a stearine candle, as reported by Zöllner* (Vol. III).

The effects of mediumistic nerve force are particularly striking in cases where there is a quick alternation of attraction and repulsion, of stronger and weaker pressure on the object, or of points impressed, as in the motions of a bow over the strings of an instrument, or in the alternate depressions of the keys of an accordion or piano, or in the guidance of a writing pencil upon a surface.† What first in these phenomena we have at present to abide by, is that they usually only occur in a circle when the chain is closed, and the playing of the accordion, as the audible writing of the pencil, immediately pauses when and as long as the chain is broken by detachment of the hand of one of the party. From this is to be understood, not only that all the party, by being charged with mediumistic nerve force, co-operate in the phenomenon, but that they co-operate in it in a way differently regulated by the medium from moment to moment. For the charging of each remains at first unaltered, even if the chain is broken ; but the changing innervation impulses, by which the medium is altering at every moment the distribution of the force, lose by the interruption of the chain their path of conduction, and thereby their operation. If a closed slate, with a fragment of pencil inside, lies on the table or on the lap of one of the party, or is held by two of them, one has to represent to oneself a system of lines of attractive force, comparable to a radial net of tense elastic cords (*Gummischnüren*), which on the one side all converge upon the bit of pencil, and on the other side conduct through the chain of sitters to the middle brain of the medium as to their central spot, from which

---

"Transcendental Physics," c. 12.—Tr.

† The following is reported of Indian fakirs. In half a cocoanut shell filled with water floats a piece of cork, which is weighted below with two straight pins, and above carries a bent pin like a duck's neck. This cork duck dances in the water to the piping of a fakir several feet off, and concludes the performance by dipping under. ("Indian Jugglers and Conjurers," in the "*Ausland*," February, 1885.)

alternately now one, now others of these threads are drawn sharper.

If individual strong mediums elicit the writing at a distance for themselves alone, in order thus to obtain instructions from their somnambulic consciousness for their direction, it is to be supposed that the different parts of the medium's body, his hand holding the slate, but especially the table beneath which the slate is pressed and on which the other hand is laid, supply the place of the chain othervise formed from a number of organisms, and likewise afford sufficient points of support for the derivation of a system of concentric lines of force.

Our ordinary writing itself, by muscular movements of the hand, depends on a similar system of push and pull lines of force, with different points of support which are peripherally distributed about the pencil; but here the push and pull are conveyed by material contact, while in the slate-writing without contact both act from a distance. Even in ordinary writing our consciousness overleaps the feeling of intermediates, and projects its writing-feeling into the point of the pencil; this must also, according to psychological analogies, be the case for the feeling of the somnambulic consciousness in the writing at a distance. The somnambulic consciousness having once accustomed itself to mediate writing by a system of push and pull lines of mediumistic nerve force, the course of this innervation impulse is as easy as the analogous course of the other sort of innervation impulse in writing by involuntary muscular movements, and therefore it is not surprising that the writing at a distance succeeds just as quickly, delivering the like strokes as those of the involuntary somnambulic writing with the hand. The kind of innervation impulse must of course be different in the muscular mediation of it and in that by mediumistic nerve force, but the rhythm in the alternation of this impulse must be in both cases the same. It may, therefore, be safely asserted, that a medium must bring practice in this rhythmical alternation of the writing impulse if he will be proficient in the writing at a distance; that is, only a medium who has learned to write will be able to produce involuntary writing or that at a distance. But even a medium versed in writing must first accustom himself to the kind of innervation impulse requisite for the writing at a distance, and to the command of it; and, therefore, is it that the early attempts are so illegible, unsymmetrical, crooked, and awry, as would be the case, suppose, with the first attempt to write with the foot.*

Already the mediumistic luminous phenomena exhibit deflnite forms, yet these are rather crystalline or still inorganic forms, as crosses, stars, a bright field with glimmering points of light, more resembling electric dust figures or Chladnic sound figures than organic forms. In the writing at a distance, on the other hand, must already be admitted a system of push and pull lines, analogous to that which acts on the hand grasping a pencil in writing. Now, if we suppose such a system of push and pull lines of the nerve force acting at a distance to act, not on a hard slate-pencil, but on a stump of soft wax of the same form and size, this must exhibit the like bendings and impressions as if a human hand had attempted the same writing with a soft wax stylus.

Suppose another arrangement of the push and pull lines of mediumistic nerve force, corresponding to those relations of pressure produced by the interior of a hand stretched out flat upon an impressionable substance, then must the displacement of parts, resulting from such a dynamical system, again agree with that produced by the pressure of the hand; that is, must show the impression of an organic form, without an organic form having been materially there producing this impression. Since the dynamical effects of the mediumistic nerve force, like those of magnetism,

---

* Compare, for instance, the samples given in Owen's "Debateable Land."

penetrate unhindered every sort of matter, no material closures of impressionable surfaces could present even a difficulty to the production of such impressions. This is also in fact the case, according to Zöllner's experiments with Slade, repeated by others with private mediums. (*Ps. St.* VII., p. 387, 388.) Zöllner says that he distinctly felt the double slate twice strongly pressed against the upper part of his thigh, on which it was laying; now as impressions were found on both the interior sides, for the one impression the system of lines of force must have pressed upon the slate ; for the other impression, the slate must have been pressed or drawn against the system of lines of force.

Were it a case of actually materialised limbs, invisible to those present, the penetration of the enclosing material, or cover, would indeed be possible according to Spiritistic views, but would require an incomparably greater development of force than the impression on an open slate; the facility and rapidity with which these impressions were obtained are as much opposed to this view, as is the fact that the impression-able lid was left intact by the push and pull lines acting through it. If materialised limbs penetrated the upper slate, the layer of soot on the inner side of that slate (if not the paper on which it was spread) must have been torn away by the foot-soles penetrating the slate ; that this did not happen, that no impression of the edge of the foot, intercepted by the upper slate, was visible in the soot-layer of the latter, and that this soot-layer remained wholly intact in the process, is a sure proof that the dynamical actions are limited to the impression of definite surfaces, that the system of force lines in question is directed only to those surface impressions, that thus, in other words, in this case, the dynamical analogue is not that of a foot, but only of a *foot-sole*, *i.e.*, of a *surface* without corporeity behind it.

As the question is only of a system of lines of force with different strengths of push (of pull, if the back of

the slate is turned to the medium), there is also no reason
why the impressions obtained should resemble the
limbs of the medium, for that which prescribes
the arrangement of the lines of force is simply
phantasy in the somnambulic consciousness of the medium,
which can deviate at pleasure from the latter's own bodily
configurations. So the impressions obtained represent limbs
of the most different size and shape; a direct impressing of the
medium's own limbs appears wholly excluded, quite apart
from particular experimental arrangements, in the case, for
example, of the impression of a child's foot.

Thus impressions of organic forms, as they cannot, like
writing, have arisen by successive, but only by simultaneous
formation, are among the most striking phenomena of the
whole province, only surpassed, perhaps, by the instances
of a penetration of matter. It is the more important inasmuch
as their durable results, the impressions obtained, like the
writing obtained, afford indubitable proof that in these two
cases we have not to do with the transfer of hallucinations,
but with objective operations of the medium's energy upon
matter.

Even those who adopt the view that the pressures are of
invisible materialised limbs, must still admit that these
invisible members are then to be conceived only as
real projections of the medium's somnambulic phantasy,
that is, that their matter is borrowed from the bodily
material of the medium, their form is occasioned and
conditioned by the medium's somnambulic phantasy, and
their effectuation by the medium's unconscious willing.
Thus even were they to be regarded as material out-
growths from the organism of the medium, still they
would be nothing further than exclusive products of the
medium, to be explained by the co-operation of his
unconscious willing, his unconscious phantasy, and his
bodily organism. And the same would be the case, should
it be supposed that in the writing at a distance an invisible

material hand mediated the forces of push and pull by which the pencil is urged; such a hand also would then be nothing more than an efflorescence of the medium.

Since, moreover, such a supposition does not at all facilitate the physical explanation of the phenomena, only adding to the invisible system of push and pull forces the superfluous hypothesis of a formed, invisible, and intangible matter, it has no scientific justification, and seems to be only the involuntary psychological product of a cleaving to sensible representation.*

Finally, there remains to be mentioned the influence of the nerve force on living organisms. That sensitive plants can be hypnotised by magnetic passes of the hand is sufficiently established;† the same is true of animals, sleeping people, children, and savages, all of whom have no notion of what has been done with them. It is not at all necessary that passes with the hands, or motions with the arms, should be made; these are only aids to the transmission of the nerve force, as are, likewise, breathing upon, or fixed gaze, none of them being at all indispensable to its out-streaming or out-beaming. As little as it is necessary for a medium to charge by magnetic passes the objects to be moved, so little is this requisite in the case of a person to be hypnotised; strong magnetisers fascinate sensitives without any mediating action, and by their mere wills place them in a manifest or masked somnambulism which paralyses their conscious will, and in its stead subjects the functioning

---

* The few reports which speak of the writing of a visible spirit hand are of no weight, as they refer to dark sittings, in which the shadowy outline of a hand on self-luminous paper is said to have been indistinctly seen.—Owen : "Debateable Land."

† The furtherance of plant-growth, which is ascribed by the Indians to the mediumistic force, I mention only by the way, because I am not aware that this phenomenon has been observed in the presence of European and American mediums as a genuine process and one applicable to all stages of development. We know, however, that the physiological functions of vegetable life can be powerfully excited, as well by super-refrangible rays as by electricity and by chemical stimulants (spirit, camphor), that even in mankind a four-year-old boy can exceptionally have attained the development of a man of thirty, and that the growth of certain quick-growing vegetable germs can be artificially accelerated. Accordingly it seems well conceivable that the mediumistic force also is such a stimulant.

somnambulic consciousness to the will of the magnetiser.*
On the other hand it is not the mere will of the magnetiser
as such which elicits these phenomena in others by a pure
psychical influence, any more than it is the mere will of
the medium that, by a pure psychical influence, produces
the physical phenomena referred to in inanimate objects; but
in both cases the immediate action of the will is only to
disengage magnetic or mediumistic nerve force from the
nervous system, and to radiate it definitely upon living or
dead objects.

This liberation and directive radiation of nerve force
is under all circumstances, no matter whether the first
impulse proceeds from the will of the waking consciousness,
or from the unconscious will of the somnambulic consciousness, not a function of those parts of the brain which serve
as support to the conscious will, but of deeper-lying layers
of the brain which either coincide with those supporting
the somnambulic consciousness, or are more approximate to
them than to the first. It is, therefore, no wonder that the
development of magnetic-mediumistic nerve force is stronger
in the somnambulic than in the waking state, and that
persons who in the latter have no power of magnetising
others, develope it in somnambulism in a high degree. This
accounts for the fact that mediums first evolve sufficient
nerve force for the production of physical phenomena when
they have entered the state of a masked somnambulism,
and that especially straining and difficult phenomena are
only produced when the masked somnambulism has passed
into complete somnambulism; that is, when the waking
consciousness and the reflex-prohibitions of the brain parts
supporting it have quite desisted, and the collective vital
energy of the nervous system has concentrated itself in
the brain parts supporting the somnambulic consciousness.

As certainly as mediums in their masked or manifest

I was told in a private letter of a strolling tinker, of demoniacal aspect,
who added to his earnings by fascinating women and inducing in them the
illusion that their kettles had holes in them and pretending to repair them.

somnambulism have the disposal of an amount of nerve force, be it self-produced or be it extracted and collected from the others present, such as no magnetiser in the complete waking state has ever developed, so certainly also must their power, by means of this surpassing quantity of force, to place the spectators in a condition of open or masked somnambulism, be greater than that of any magnetiser operating in the waking state. It is a common phenomenon at mediumistic sittings for sensitive members of them to fall into swoons, convulsions, trance, ecstacy or hypnosis, and these phenomena would be much more frequent if the mediums had an interest in them, and therefore sought to motive their unconscious wills to elicit them. Mediums, however, have just the contrary interest, opposed to the occurrence of open somnambulism among the spectators, because this has usually a disturbing effect being often accompanied by convulsions and the like, which divert the attention of the rest from them and their performances, and they may find in the new somnambules competing mediums who may arbitrarily counteract their dispositions of the nerve force present in the circle.

On the other hand, mediums may well have an interest in eliciting a masked somnambulism in the party collectively to the degree that they are thus made susceptible to the transference of hallucinations, without becoming at the same time qualified for active competition with the medium. This interest and the nature of its motivation need not, of course, occur to the consciousness of mediums. But when it is considered that a somnambulic medium has hallucinations which he takes for reality, and has at the same time the lively wish that the spectators should perceive the same supposed reality, that is, have the same (hallucinatory) representations as himself, evidently we have given in the medium all sufficient psychological conditions to compel him to an unconscious influencing of the spectators, in the sense that they are placed in a condition favourable to the arising of like representations (*i.e.*, to the infection o hallucinations), which is just the condition of masked somnambulism.

Now since already, in masked somnambulism, mediums are actually subject to hallucinations of all sorts, usually without knowing them as such ; since, in open somnambulism, they are wholly possessed by them ; since, further, on account of their vocation, and from considerations of business, they, in fact, wish that the reality recognised by them of such purely subjective phenomena should also be recognised by those present; it would be inexplicable if, with the combination of conditions so favourable, the instatement of masked somnambulism in the assembled party, with frequent infection of the medium's hallucinations, did not occur.

If, in Spiritistic circles, these facts have yet not been at all remarked and regarded, that is because the concern has been only on behalf of the objective reality of all phenomena, so that such an observation from another quarter exasperates, and is rejected as a sacrilege. From the scientific psychological standpoint, on the other hand, every participator in mediumistic sittings must constantly regard himself as under the influence of a very strong magnetiser, whose unconscious interest it is to place him in masked somnambulism, for infection of hallucinations, and must consider that this influence is the more powerful the oftener he has frequented mediumistic sittings, and the oftener he has sat with the same medium. He must say to himself that this state of a masked somnambulism is announced to his own waking consciousness by no direct symptom, but only by the capacity for being infected by the representations, especially the sensations, and quite particularly the hallucinations of the magnetiser (here the medium), and must be the more prepared for implanted hallucinations, the longer he occupies himself practically with the subject.

We shall see later on how extensively this transference of hallucinations actually takes places at mediumistic sittings ; at present we are only establishing the fàct, that in a circle of similar composition,throughout a long series of sittings, the most favourable conditions conceivable are afforded for elicitation of a masked somnambulism even in non-sensitive persons.

III.

The Ideality of the Manifestations (*Der Vorstellungsinhalt der Kundgebungen*).

Having in the previous section discussed the phenomena, which more or less serve as the expression of an ideal content, or under favourable circumstances are applicable to the communication of it, we have now to examine the ideal content itself, which is communicated to us in these unusual ways. Already in dealing with the involuntary movements of speaking, writing, &c., we saw that the guiding intelligence is to be sought in the somnambulic consciousness of the medium ; but as the handwriting remains the same, whether the pencil is guided by involuntary muscular movements of the hand itself, or by the mediumistic nerve force through a system of dynamical push and pull lines, so the content of the writing remains in both cases the same. We have, therefore, no reason whatever to doubt that the same parts of the brain which give the innervation-impulse for the radiation and distribution of the nerve force, as for the involuntary muscular movements, serve also for the support of the somnambulic consciousness.

The ideality of the manifestations of a "speaking-

medium " coincides with the temporary ideality of his somnambulic consciousness ; for a speaking medium is only an
auto-somnambule with the peculiarity of spontaneously imparting his occasional ideas connectedly. The ideality of a
writing-medium is, however, not essentially different from
that of a speaking-medium, and that of the former is independent of the mode of writing, whether by rapping out
the alphabet, or by pointing out letters, or by involuntary
handwriting, or by writing at a distance. Whether the
medium speaks with changed voice, writes with changed
handwriting, or speaks or writes in the character of a named
or unnamed third person, makes no difference in this
conception ; for we know that in the somnambulic consciousness a conversion of the *Ego* into another person is a
phenomenon of quite common occurrence.

Since the medium is either without waking consciousness, or if in masked somnambulism his persisting waking
consciousness has ordinarily no knowledge of what passes
in the somnambulic consciousness, the medium also must
be unaware that it is himself—his somnambulic consciousness—who has in himself, and ejects from himself, this ideal
content, *i.e.*, he writes in his waking capacity unconsciously. The experimental proof that this writing is only
relatively unconscious, but for the masked somnambulic
consciousness is conscious, may, however, be afforded by
the medium placing himself in open somnambulism, and
then remembering the former unconscious writing and
giving an account of it by word of mouth. This happened
with Slade, for example, according to Zöllner's report, in
respect of a writing at a distance effected in a closed slate
the previous day, which had not yet been opened, so that
none of the party knew the contents.*

The writing or other mechanical means can give information of everything comprehended in the medium's
somnambulic consciousness, but of nothing which this does

---

* " Transcendental Physics," c. 10.

not fathom. The ideality of the manifestations is just so instructed or ignorant, cultured or uncultured, serious or sportive, thoughtful or foolish, witty or dull, intellectual or silly, as is the content of the medium's somnambulic consciousness. There is no longer much dispute about that; but there are still individuals who are unable to keep distinguished the somnambulic and waking contents of the medium's consciousness, and refer the deviations of the former from the latter to a source apart from the entire person of the medium. It is thus really the ignorance or insufficient knowledge of somnambulism which causes Spiritists to misapprehend the obvious exclusive origin of the communications.

The masked somnambulic consciousness compasses the simultaneously existing waking consciousness, without being itself compassed by the latter, as the waking consciousness of the past is compassed by the consciousness of open somnambulism, but not the converse. In other words : the conduction of ideas and wishes from the parts of the brain supporting the waking consciousness into those supporting the somnambulic consciousness is easy, but the reverse is difficult. Therefore it is, that the somnambulic consciousness writes words and sentences, answers questions, and takes account of wishes, dictated and proposed by the waking consciousness, either before the commencement of the masked somnambulism or during its continuance. On the other hand, however, the somnambulic consciousness is also able to answer such questions and to heed such wishes as have become known to it (e.g., by thought-reading), though not to the waking consciousness.

The content of the somnambulic consciousness is distinguished from that of waking consciousness partly by its form, partly by its derivation. The form is generally more perceptional (anschaulichen) of greater sensuous palpability, inclines to symbolising and personifications, but is thus easily confused, obscure, and enigmatical in comparison with the abstract reflections of waking consciousness. The derivation is partly the simultaneous waking consciousness, partly the hyperæsthetic memory of the parts of the brain supporting somnambulism, partly direct Thought-transference,* and finally, in part, true clairvoyance. Whoever rightly knows the range of these different sources will scarcely be tempted to look beyond them for explanation of the ideal content of the mediumistic manifestations. But unfortunately the facts of the hyperæsthesia of memory, transference of conscious and unconscious impressions, and clairvoyance are, to the great majority of Spiritists, as unknown as to their opponents. So far, however, as they are known, they are deliberately thrust aside and under-estimated, because they threaten destruction to the wishes of the heart.

Hyperæsthetic memory of the somnambulic consciousness yields often the most astonishing material, the derivation of which seems wholly inexplicable, because the simultaneous waking consciousness of the medium has not only no memory of this material, but often fallaciously believes itself able to conclude from accessory circumstances that such impressions could never have been experienced by it. As the somnambulic speaking is able to repeat the sound of words or sentences in foreign, not understood, languages, which have been heard long ago without attention, so can the somnambulic writing repeat the written or printed characters of words and sentences in languages not understood, which have been once regardlessly seen, or even spell such out from unintelligent memory of word-sounds in languages not quite unknown. If, besides, in

* *Vorstellungsübertragung* I translate "Thought-transference," because that term is already familiar to the English reader, who is in no danger of here restricting "thought" to intellectual process, or a purely abstract content. "*Vorstellung*" is sometimes rendered "idea" (as by Messrs. Haldane and Kemp in the title of (and throughout) Schopenhauer's work); "idea" having, then, the extended significance which Berkeley gave to it. In its most general sense, "*Vorstellung*" is perhaps most properly translated "representation," as always by Mr. Meiklejohn in his translations of Kant's "Critique of Pure Reason." Dr. Hutchison Stirling, in his "Secret of Hegel," remarks on the frequent difficulty of finding a good English equivalent.—Tr.

such proceeding the symbolising and personifying tendency of the somnambulic consciousness induces it to put these communications in the mouth of an absent person, its dramatic metamorphosising talent must at the same time succeed in dressing out the communication with all sorts of small external traits appropriate to the person represented. In this way communications can be brought about, which in form and content appear to belong as little as possible to the waking consciousness of the medium, and as much as possible to the supposed author of the dictation. Anyone not familiar with the peculiarities of the somnambulic consciousness will in such case almost unavoidably fall into the delusion that the communications are under the spiritual influence of the absent or deceased person who is indicated in them as their author.*

Thought-transference yields results which, for those who are unacquainted with this class of facts, are still more surprising than the effects of hyperæsthesia of memory.† We are here putting quite aside interpretation by attitude, gesture, involuntary muscular movements, &c., although even this interpretation may be involuntary, instinctive, of reflex manifestation (*reflektorisch zur Kundgebung gelangende*), and from the latter afterwards first recognised by the waking consciousness. We restrict ourselves rather to the cases in which such sort of mediation is undoubtedly excluded by the experimental arrangements. We have, then, to distinguish (1) willed perception with willed implantation ; (2) willed perception without will in the other to implant ; (3) not willed perception with will to implant ; (4) not willed perception without will in the other to implant. The will to implant on the side of the person

---

* Of this nature, for example, seem to me mainly Aksakow's " Philological Problems mediumistically propounded." (*Ps. St.*, X., 547 ; XI, 1, 49, *et seq.*)

† Compare the opportune survey of this subject by Du Prel : " Das Gedankenlesen " (" Thought-reading "), Breslau: Schottländer. 1885. Especially pp. 11-13, 16-18, 28-30.

transmitting,* and the will to apprehend on that of the recipient, are powerful furtherances to thought-transference ; and, indeed, the will to implant seems to have an incomparably greater power of realisation than the will to perceive : a power so great, that with persons in sympathetic *rapport* through love, friendship, or magnetic relations, it overcomes all earthly distance. The will to perception of others' thoughts can also act favourably, but not in the same degree as the will to implant, because perception by the waking consciousness is generally impossible, and the somnambulic consciousness is not immediately subject to the conscious will ; more operative than the latter is the ardent desire of the heart, the inward and urgent longing, because it imparts itself to and intensifies the somnambulic will.

The will to implant operates likewise, at least in proximity, only through an excitation of the somnambulic parts of the brain ; but this active, and in few seconds concentrated, excitation is more easily directed, than is the passive to perception, since to a brief percipient excitation there may be no corresponding energetic thought whatever in the other. The will to implant may also be an unconcious one, seated in the somnambulic layers of the brain, in so far as the urgent heart-longing produces the wish to be perceptible to a beloved person ; so sleepers may have this unconscious will and transmit their dream-images to a distant person awake or likewise dreaming. With extinction of the motive feelings (home-sickness, longing of love), usually disappears also the unconscious will to thought implantation. All reports of voluntary implantation of intuitive representations in a distant person point to this, that the success of such experiments depends as much on the ability of the willer to place himself transitorily in open or masked somnambulism, as on the sensitivity of the

---

* The "agent" in the convenient terminology of Messrs. Gurney and Myers in the publications of the Society for Psychical Research. This term (and the correlative "percipient") not being restricted to the case of *voluntary* processes, might be used here throughout, could I venture to take such a liberty with the text.—TR.

recipient and the strength of the sympathetic *rapport* between the two. The result seems easier, when the recipient is in a dreaming or half-awake condition, in one, that is, in which the waking consciousness is more or less suppressed.

Success seems most sure when two persons agree upon a definite minute in which to direct their thoughts upon each other, both placing themselves in open or masked somnambulism, the stronger willing of the two undertaking the active, the more sensitive the passive part. If two persons have first practised this distant intercourse, the connection between them is to be re-established at any time by the will of one being directed on the other, exciting in the latter at first an indefinite feeling, or appearance of a distant light, or some other indication serving as a signal, and occasioning him to place himself in somnambulism, for the perception of definite communications (*Vorstellungen*). In this way the initiates of higher degrees in the secret brotherhoods of Tibet have acquired the power of conversing with one another at a distance without telegraph wires, and similar attempts have often succeeded in Europe.* They are most hopeful between magnetiser and somnambule, if the magnetiser is able to put himself into open or masked somnambulism.

Persons between whom there is no sympathetic *rapport* will have no prospect of success in thought-transference at great distances ; in this case the transference, if it is to succeed at all, must be facilitated by spatial proximity or material connection. The nearer the two are to each other in the same room, the better success is there, while in the transference over extended tracts the degree of remoteness does not signify. The presence of other persons is disturbing, because then the cross-influence of all their thoughts trouble and confuse the particular thought to be perceived ;

* Cf. *Ps. St.*, VII., 481-488 ; VI., 294-301, 344-352 ; Du Prel's " Thought-reading," p. 24-26.

and it is especially necessary that spectators should stand considerably away from the transferor. Also confronting with eyes bound seems better for success than when one stands behind the other. If several agree to think the same thought, the transference is facilitated, as the number is greater, evidently by a multiplication or exaltation of the influence similar to that attained when the will to implant and the intensity of the thought are strengthened in a single individual.

Contact, as by application of forehead to forehead, laying the hand on the forehead, crown, or back of the head, or clasping hands, facilitates greatly ; but as here the influence of unconscious understanding of involuntary muscular movements comes already into play, results thus obtained no longer prove immediate thought-transference. It is better to form a chain of hands between the two persons, yet then the intermediates introduce disturbance, positive results being only still obtained when the recipient is somnambulic, and in magnetic relation to the transferor, but in no *rapport* with the intervening persons. (*Ps. St.* IV., 298.) I cannot understand why inorganic conductors of different substances (metal wires, damp cords, &c.) have not yet been used in these experiments, as every communication by involuntary muscular movements is securely avoided by such interposition. Between magnetiser and somnambule no contact or conduction is required to transfer the sense impressions and thoughts of the former to the latter. (*Ps. St.* III., 529-531.) Also light seems to have a disturbing influence in these experiments, which may bear out the corresponding assertion of mediums ; moreover all fatigue is to be carefully avoided, and series of from 30 to 100 experiments in immediate succession, such as Richet's, are a mistake.*

* [*Revue Philosophique* for December, 1884. The English reader will also find an account of these experiments in the number for December, 1884, of the *Proceedings* of the Society for Psychical Research (Trübner, Ludgate-hill, E.C.). The important original experiments of this Society, recorded in various numbers of its *Proceedings* during the past three years, should be referred to in connection with this subject.—TR.]

As regards the nature of the representations, the most easily transferable appear to be feelings, dispositions, and distinct sensations of the lower sense organs. Transference of musical impressions and their combinations seems not yet to have been tried, although the telephone, as an aid to sensible presentation, would facilitate such experiments ; the diviner must, of course, be musical enough to designate or imitate the tune heard. The transference of visual representations is easier as the representation approximates by hallucinatory distinctness and vivacity to perception ; perhaps the facilitation of transference at a distance when the transferor is in a somnambulic state has for its sole reason the fact that only in this state are hallucinatory distinctness and vivacity possible. The transference of whatever is not sensible perception or its lively reproduction will be much more difficult, but still in that case easiest when it is clothed with the perceptional form of inwardly spoken and heard words.

All transferences at a distance are hallucinatory sight-pictures, usually of the figure itself of the person who would be manifest to beloved ones at a distance. I know no case in which words put in the mouth of such a figure by the phantasy of the recipient have been verified by the transferor. All manifestations at a distance are completed by mimical movements of the implanted hallucinations, or by symbolical additions to them, but abstract thoughts are never transferred at such a distance.

In immediate proximity, under favourable conditions, not only words, sentences and numbers, but also abstract thoughts, and even thoughts not clothed in words, are transferable. Somnambules accomplish with tolerable certainty the thought-commands of the magnetiser (*Ps. St.*VI. 103-106), especially if used to this sort of transference; they can repeat, by writing and verbally, words and sentences in languages which they do not understand, which the magnetiser or another placed in *rapport* with him, dictates for transference, and even understand the sense of them, so far as the transferor understands and conceives while speaking the words aloud or inwardly. The proof is in the fact that somnambules answer intelligently, in languages with which they are familiar, questions put in languages of which they are ignorant, but the answer fails as soon as the question is put in a language which the questioner himself does not understand.* Here it is clear that a thought is transferred which is intelligible by itself, apart from the words, unintelligible to the somnambule, to which it is attached ; this is the most spiritualised case of thought-transference conceivable.

When there is neither the conscious nor unconscious will to transfer a mental representation, but there is on the other side the conscious or unconscious will to perceive, then the usually too-widely employed term "thought-reading" is strictly applicable; in which is included " character-reading." A somnambule who is placed in *rapport* with a person previously quite unknown to him, either by direct contact, or by the mediation of the magnetiser, or by contact with an object containing the personal aura of the individual in question, receives a certain collective impression of the latter, a compound of impressions sympathetic and antipathetic. If now the somnambule's will is directed to the interpretation, dissection, and restoration of this impression, there will emerge, according to the sensitivity, and faculty of conveying its impressions in words, a more or less incomplete, indefinite, and inexact, yet not wholly unlike picture of the personality, its character, its immediate feelings and dispositions, and under circumstances even its immediate thought. Thought-reading can finally be an involuntary reception of impressions, if the sensitivity of the somnambule is highly exalted, and the other conditions are favourable.

The percipient of the transferred representations is

---

* Du Prel : "Das Gedankenlesen," (Thought-Reading), pp. 19-22.

always the somnambulic consciousness, never immediately the waking consciousness. If the somnambulic consciousness is alone present and commands the machinery of speech, it is not difficult to establish by interrogation the fact that thought-transference has taken place. It is otherwise if the percipient's somnambulic consciousness is masked by the waking consciousness, and the latter has sole rule over the organs of speech and the voluntary muscles. In such cases it cannot be said whether behind the waking consciousness there is a somnambulic consciousness or not, and whether, if there is, it perceives another's thoughts or not. Only when the division between somnambulic and waking consciousness is not complete, but a faint shimmer of the somnambulic consciousness gleams unnoticed into the waking consciousness, imparting a weak colouring to the contents of the latter : only then is it possible to infer mediately, from the waking consciousness, that a thought-transference has taken place in the somnambulic consciousness.

The waking consciousness of a normal person must thus be consulted as to the representations in the other person's mind, and if in a long series of experiments its testimony is better than was to be expected from the calculation of probabilities, the overplus is to be set to the credit of the thought-reading somnambulic consciousness which even in the normal person lies concealed. These experiments are instituted by Richet,* and in the guessing of colours of playing cards have yielded about ten per cent. better results than the probability, experimental results when the cards were drawn without being looked at agreeing with the latter. Had results when the brain was tired not been taken into account, the percentage in favour of an influence upon the waking by the somnambulic consciousness would have been considerably larger. It is most desirable that the experiments should be repeated with avoidance of

* " La Suggestion Mentale et le Calcul des Probabilités,"*Revue Philosophique,* 1884, No. 12, pp. 609-674. 1885, No. 1, pp. 115-118.

all fatigue and with greater exclusion of light, new experiments being added by introducing a conductor between the two bodies, gradually increasing the number of transferors, and varying the distance between them and the diviner.

With sensitives to experiment upon, there is a very different prospect of results. Whereas in normal persons the somnambulic consciousness not only remains below the threshold, but also has small noticeable influence on the content of the waking consciousness, with sensitives this influence is remarkably apparent, and can be considerably exalted by avoidance of every disturbing and distracting external impression on the waking consciousness, and by attention being concentrated on stimulations transmitted from the somnambulic sphere. Barrett's experiments on healthy but sensitive children show that the successful cases of transference of perceptional thoughts (*e.g.*, objects to be fetched) from a person thinking them to the sensitive may exceed the probable figure by more than 100 per cent., and that in the transference by several persons fixing on the same thought the chances of success may rise almost to certainty, so that the sensitive already guessed while outside the room the thought of the sitters within.*

Still more favourable are the conditions, if the difficulties of transition of the thought from the somnambulic into the waking consciousness are avoided, *i.e.*, if the experimental conditions are so arranged that the persisting waking consciousness knows nothing at all of the guessing and announcing. This is possible, if the reflex-prohibitions of the parts of the brain supporting the waking consciousness are so far debilitated as to admit the despatch of involuntary innervation impulses by the parts of the brain supporting the somnambulic consciousness. This happens in the state of masked somnambulism when the somnambulic

---

* Barrett, Professor of Physics at the Royal College of Science, Ireland. "On Thought-Reading." *Ps. St.* [The English reader will find Professor Barrett's contributions to the subject in the first vol. of the *Proceedings* of the Society for Psychical Research.—TR.]

consciousness, veiled by the waking consciousness, announces its contents either by involuntary muscular movements,* or by mediumistic nerve force. Already the divining rod is even for apparently normal and insensitive persons an excellent aid for revealing the thoughts of others by involuntary designation, so far as these thoughts are fixed on an object in the room, and yields successful results exceeding the probable figure about two to three-fold. (*Revue Phil.*, 1884. No. 12, p. 639, *et seq.*)†

Yet more surprising are the results if recourse be had to the table, for rapping, or to the psychograph, requiring, it is true, longer practice than the divining rod. Involuntary writing with the hand leaves too much room for interchange with voluntary writing and for the suspicion of intentional deception, for it to be suitable for demonstrative experiments; but in the writing at a distance of mediums, excluding the change into voluntary writing, there is the purest possible experimental material, which then, as indubitable expression of the masked somnambulic consciousness, affords also, in fact, the most astonishing proofs of thought-reading. If, for instance, questions are written in a closeable slate, on the second inner side of which the medium then writes at a distance the answers (*Ps. St.* IV. 388; XI. 497),‡ no explanation more readily suggests itself than that the somnambulic consciousness of the medium perceives the question from the thought of the person writing it down, and thereupon imparts the answer.

Thought-reading is yet more involved and removed from detection, in that not only thoughts of the waking consciousness, but even those of the masked somnambulic

---

* ["We have in our collection," says Mr. Edmund Gurney, "several cases where a mental question, on the part of some one present, has been answered in writing, either with a *planchette* or a simple pencil, without any consciousness of either the question or the answer on the part of the person whose hand was automatically acting." *Proceedings* of the Society for Psychical Research. December, 1884.—Tr.]

† IM. Richet himself, as diviner, thus obtained 6 successes in 13 trials, the probability being 1 in 6. *Proceedings* of the Society for Psychical Research, December, 1884. P. 245.—Tr.]

‡ [An experiment which is said to have repeatedly succeeded also with the medium Eglinton.—Tr.]

consciousness of the persons present, can make entry into the somnambulic consciousness of the medium. This could only be completely proved by experimenting with two mediums, one to guess the answers which the other had made to questions without previous knowledge by the waking consciousness. But it can also be inferred with approximate certainty from the fact that somnambules frequently give information concerning the past of the questioner, contradicting the present recollections of his waking consciousness, that the statement is nevertheless persisted in, and that either his memory, sharpened by more circumstantial additions, at once recognises his own error, or being subsequently accidentally led into the right track confirms the somnambule's assertion.* Such cases are usually treated as clairvoyance, but it seems more probable that there is a masked somnambulic memory in the questioner, which, excited by the question, by means of its hyperæsthesia realises truer recollections than the duller memory of waking consciousnesss. Further, some-one present, whose interest is excited in a particular direction, may have in his masked somnambulic conscious-ness recollections of formerly heard or seen sentences in foreign languages; these impressions may, by the medium, be divined by thought-reading and be involuntarily written (or rapped out), without the waking consciousness of the other recognising the result thus presented to him as his own recollections.†

As these instances are not numerous, and as on the other hand there are a not inconsiderable percentage of persons, in whom the masked somnambulic consciousness lying below the threshold has a certain vivacity, nothing is opposed to the presumption that the phenomenon in question only occurs in somnambules in connection with such persons having masked somnambulic consciousness.

* Du Prel's "Thought-reading," pp. 22, 23.
† Cf. Aksakow's already cited " Philological Problems mediumistically propounded."

Given the case of the somnambulic and waking consciousnesses of the questioner presenting their respective impressions
of different characters to the somnambule, according to the
foregoing it is not surprising that the more hallucinatory
impression of the somnambulic consciousness is easier perceived than the more abstract thoughts of the waking
consciousness, so that under these suppositions the phenomenon also is explained without clairvoyance

Slade, for example, saw the figures which were on the
three coins contained in the plastered-up boxes, and Zöllner
finds in that an instance of true clairvoyance, because he
had put the coins in the boxes a long time previously, and no
longer exactly remembered of what description they were.*
Just in this case it seems to me doubtless, though subsequent
confirmation by correction of Zöllner's memory is wanting,
that there was here no clairvoyance, but thought-reading of
somnambulic impressions. For that Zöllner was a masked
somnambule, who, without knowing it, co-operated with
Slade, is highly probable from the whole character of the
phenomena manifested in those sittings, and just as
probable is it that Zöllner, in putting up the coins, had accurately observed them. These two suppositions suffice,
however, for the data, first, that Zöllner's somnambulic
memory had taken in the numbers of the coins, and secondly,
that with the tension of mental occupation with the object,
the hyperæsthetic somnambulic memory realised these
numbers, while the memory of the waking consciousness
endeavoured in vain to recall even the descriptions of the
coins. Under such circumstances, Slade's somnambulic
consciousness could perceive the numbers by thought-
transference, and all that is striking in the case is that this

---

* ["Transcendental Physics," c.IX. Zöllner's statement is as follows :—
As mentioned above, I had already, in December, 1877 " (the séance was on
the 5th May, 1878)," fastened up these boxes, and as I had observed neither the
value of the enclosed coins nor their dates, I could afterwards only ascertain by
the noise from shaking the boxes, that enclosed in the circular one was a large
German coin (a thaler or a five-mark piece), in the rectangular one two smaller
pieces ; whether these were pennies, groschen, or five-groschen pieces, I had,
after the lapse of half-a-year, at the time of Slade's last stay in Leipzig, entirely
forgotten." Page 155 (English translation).—TR.]

perception was so lively as to pass as visionary sight into the waking consciousness and into expression there ; unless the opinion is preferred, that at that moment Slade's waking consciousness had sunk below the threshold, and the somnambulic had possessed itself of the organs of speech. Slade being also a speaking medium, there is nothing to prevent the adoption of the latter view.

A medium has always a lively interest in divining the open or masked thoughts of those present ; for it is his interest to educe astonishing manifestations, and nothing can be more astonishing for "sound common-sense " (" *gesunden Menschen verstand* ") than exhibitions of a knowledge which the persons present believe to be confined exclusively to themselves, or which is even withdrawn from their own waking consciousness. The will to perceive must therefore be supposed continually present in the medium. But if the others, on their side likewise, have a lively interest in the occurrence of striking phenomena, that must develope in them the will to support the medium according to their own powers, and to lighten his difficulties. And then the unconscious will is excited to thought-transference. Moreover in circles the hands are in contact, so that all conditions are as favourable as possible for thought-transference. And when the other person is a masked somnambule like Zöllner, it is scarcely still surprising that results at such sittings should exceed the average.

For experiments in intentional thought-transference, there can be no subjects better adapted than mediums with the faculty of writing at a distance, only there must be an end to misusing the medium's nerve force by the childish game of oracular questioning, and systematic experimentation must take its place. These trials must at first relate to impressions of single senses, and gradually rise to more abstract representations ; the distance of the transferor from the medium must also be gradually increased, and the percentage of successes as depending on distance be ascertained. For the effects at greater (mile-wide) distances, a second medium must be introduced, and the influence of distance, if any, and of what kind, must be determined. Hitherto spiritistic sittings afford no material for thought-transference at great distance, the medium having always been the only active party, instead of being reduced, as in such experiments is necessary, to a passive relation to another medium at a distant place.

Du Prel goes still further, conceiving that thought-reading extends not only to representations actually present in somnambulic consciousness, but even to latent memory. (*Gedankenlesen*, p. 22.) As proof, he adduces the faculty of different individuals (of whom some are "possessed" persons, some Church dignitaries, some ordinary persons, like Zschokke) of seeing perceptibly before them the crises of another's life on first sight of him or hearing his voice. Du Prel here proceeds on the supposition that the actual somnambulic consciousness is at the same time the latent memory of the waking consciousness, and has thus only to meet the difficulty, how from the simultaneous medley of all important and unimportant memories in the somnambulic consciousness, the more important should be read out in orderly succession.* As I ascribe to the somnambulic, as to the waking consciousness, only particular actual representations, and besides, a latent material of memory in molecular predispositions of the parts of the brain supporting the consciousness, I must suppose a clairvoyant transference of molecular brain-predispositions, unless there remains the expedient that the thought-reader, by his unconscious will to perception of character and fate, magnetically constrains the somnambulic consciousness of the other to recollection of the crises of

---

* [For a full exposition of Du Prel's views, the reader should be referred to his "Philosophie der Mystik," my translation of which is now nearly complete, and will, I hope, before long be published.—TR.]

his life, and perceives them thus actualised in memory.* This view is, in my opinion, always preferable, that the seer is excited by the *rapport* of sense established with the other person, clairvoyantly to restore out of himself the events of that person's life, with the scenes of some crisis in it.

The distinction between clairvoyance and thought-reading is that in the latter only present thoughts of waking, dreaming, or somnambulic persons are perceived, by a certain resonance of the percipient's own somnambulic consciousness, while in the former not only the contents of another consciousness, but real objective phenomena as such are perceived without normal mediation of the instruments of sense.† The exclusion of perception by the normal five senses by no means excludes every sort of influence upon sense, but this influence acts neither on sight, hearing, smell, taste, nor touch, but on the sensitive feeling, whose perceptions are then first changed by the somnambulic consciousness into representations of sight, or hearing, or thought. Most easily explainable is the sensitive feeling of the personal emanations of men or animals, perception of unobserved cats, designation among several glasses of water of the one in which a finger has been dipped (*Ps. St.*, X., 113, 114, 255-257), because here there need be no change into the perceptional form of one of the five senses, the idea immediately presenting itself. The explanation becomes more difficult when a somnambule, by feeling, correctly names the time shown by a watch set at random and placed in a box, the somnambule applying the object to the side of the head and then believing himself, as it were, to see (III., 532), or when he reads the mottos, enclosed in nuts shortly before bought, and known to none of the party

---

* Zschokke: "Eine Selbstscnau" (An Introspect), Aarau. Sauerländer. 1842. Vol.I., pp. 273-276.

† This distinction between thought-reading and clairvoyance has been already insisted upon by Gregory in his "Letters on Animal Magnetism" (1851), but up to the present has been insufficiently regarded. (Compare Wallace, "The Scientific Aspect of the Supernatural.")

(IV., 299). Still more complicated is the case when the magnetiser places a finger on a chance unknown word in a newspaper, and the word is given by the somnambule ;* here, to escape true clairvoyance, it has to be supposed that the somnambulic consciousness of the magnetiser perceived the word through his finger, and that the somnambule received it by thought-transference. Yet further is the difficulty increased when a medium, by writing at a distance, copies a page, chosen at random, of a closed book laid under the table, although at mediumistic sittings a considerable extension of the medium's sphere of sensitive perception is to be expected.

Nearer again to true clairvoyance are the cases in which the sensitive feeling serves only to establish *rapport*, to direct the somnambulic consciousness to this point or object among an infinite number of possible ones, but not as substitute for sense-perception, *i.e.*, for transmission of the collective mental contents. When, for instance, a somnambule, from the feeling of a lock of hair, defines the particular pains and the character of the disease from which the distant and unknown person is suffering, or by a bit of elephant's tooth which had been found under lava, is excited to visions of troops of elephants and volcanic eruptions, or when a sensitive, disposed to hallucinations, is excited by the drop of coagulated blood lying under the flooring of a bedroom to visions of a suicide or murder,

---

* [See Crookes' "Notes of an Inquiry into the Phenomena called Spiritual." "A lady was writing automatically by means of the planchette. I was trying to devise a means of proving that what she wrote was not due to 'unconscious cerebration.' The planchette, as it always does, insisted that, although it was moved by the hand and arm of the lady, the *intelligence* was that of an invisible being who was playing on her brain as on a musical instrument, and thus moving her muscles. I, therefore, said to this intelligence, 'Can you see the contents of this room?' 'Yes,' wrote the planchette. 'Can you see to read this newspaper?' said I, putting my finger on a copy of the *Times*, which was on a table behind me, but without looking at it. 'Yes,' was the reply of the planchette. 'Well,' I said, 'if you can see that, write the word which is now covered by my finger, and I will believe you.' The planchette commenced to move. Slowly, and with great difficulty, the word 'however' was written. I turned round, and saw that the word 'however' was covered by the tip of my finger. I had purposely avoided looking at the newspaper when I tried this experiment, and it was impossible for the lady, had she tried, to have seen any of the printed words, for she was sitting at one table and the paper was on another table behind, my body intervening."—TR.]

agreeing with the past facts, to him unknown, of this place, or when someone by involuntary writing sets down with substantial, if not verbal, fidelity the three hundred years old poetical dedication of a spinet, afterwards first discovered hidden in the clefts of the latter;* in all these cases clairvoyance is at work. Yet in all these instances the possibility of unconscious sensitive reconstruction of causes from felt effects is still comparatively large ; for we do not at all know to what degree of subtlety the traces of past events are stored up in their remains, and can be felt out by a highly sensitive person.

On the other hand, sense-mediation vanishes to an unassignable minimum, when instead of sensitive perception by feeling, an interest of the will takes over the establishment of *rapport*, *e.g.*, a strong love or friendship, or a mighty patriotism and home sympathy. The seeing at a distance of great natural events in a remote country (fires, earthquakes, war) might still, so far as simultaneous, be referred to thought-reading in the consciousness of persons present at them, and explanation of vision into futurity might be sought in unconscious inference from present circumstances known by thought-reading, since present circumstances contain as well the germ of the future as the deposit of the past. But this interpretation is very difficult with regard to events not within the single course of one train of causes, but arising through unexpected intersection of causal series seemingly lying far apart from each other.†

A corpse-seer, that is to say, one who dreaming or awake foresees cases of death among his acquaintance or at home, may also infer from feelings of serious illness known by thought-reading, that death is at hand, or from dispositions of a person in health known by thought-reading, that there is a tendency to suicide. But why, in that case,

---

* Owen's "Debateable Land."
† Compare Du Prel : "Second Sight" (Breslau : Schottländer. 1883, Preis 50 Pf.), pp. 13-18.

does not that which thought-reading immediately apprehends emerge into the waking or dreaming consciousness, why first an inference from that? And why are so often just the unessential details of the death or funeral foreseen? How, from the present contents of another consciousness, is to be got the fact, for instance, that just such a place in the city will be chosen for the suicidal shot, or that this particular horse will shy, rear, fling off, and fatally injure the healthy rider? How is to be explained the case of a lady seeing from the window a funeral with well-known mourners drawn through her garden, never used for the passage of funerals, but which yet, some days later, in consequence of a flooding of the road, has to be opened in fact for the passage of the foreseen funeral procession? How can the knowledge of any number of people's thoughts help to prevision, in the place or neighbourhood of their occurrence, of impending fires caused by lightning, or by other events arising accidentally, *i.e.*, out of remote series of causes?

In such cases there seems to be neither mediation by sense nor a possible reduction to thought-reading, and the *rapport* seems simply conditioned by interest for friends or home. In such cases have we first undoubtedly to do with pure clairvoyance, which always appears in hallucinatory form,* if also frequently with symbolical investment. Just this sort of " second-sight," however, is far more frequent than is supposed, and by confidential inquiry there will be found in a very large percentage of families a corpse-seeress or ghost-seeress, or the tradition of one. This true clairvoyance can therefore depend neither on thought-reading nor on any sort of sensitive apprehension of ether-vibrations, but must be recognised as a faculty of spiritual overleaping space and time. Thereby is the hallucination, which announces the future to consciousness, evidently only the last result of

---

* There can be hallucinations of hearing as of sight ; *e.g.*, prevision of a conflagration may be by hearing of the fire-bells and alarms, or the foreknowledge may clothe itself in the heard words of a phantasm.

absolutely unconscious psychical processes, which as such need no sense or material mediation.

Confronted with such facts, either one concedes to the individual soul the faculty of absolute knowledge— that is, of knowledge unlimited by time and space, or one goes behind the individual soul to its essential root in the absolute spirit ; in both cases no external and no intermediate assistance is any longer wanted, least of all by spirits of the departed, who also are still only individual souls.

In the first case, the monads or individuals are divided from their absolute ground, from which they yet necessarily must have sprouted, and a property is ascribed to them which only attaches to and beseems the absolute ; the other case suggests the inseverable navel-string connecting every creature with its all-mother nature, and the reflection that also in this navel-string spiritual saps must circulate, of which consciousness has only no usual apprehension. If all individuals of higher or lower order are rooted in the Absolute, retrogressively in this they have a second connection among themselves, and there is requisite only a restoration of the *rapport* or telephonic junction (*Telephonanschluss*) between two individuals in the Absolute, by an intense interest of the will, to bring about the unconscious spiritual interchange between them without sense-mediation. The hyperæsthesia of the parts of the brain supporting the somnambulic consciousness makes inspiration from the absolutely unconscious (immaterial) psychical functions of the particular individual soul much easier than does the normal excitability of the parts of the brain supporting waking consciousness. The absolutely unconscious functions of the individual soul are, however, *eo ipso* again functions of the absolute subject as of one limited, and the strong interest of the will serves for motivation of such unconscious functions, which act inspirationally on the somnambulic consciousness.

In the absolute consciousness of the absolute spirit all the threads of causal series are ideally entwined to a single collective intuition, so that from it is predeterminable even what appears accidental in the events of the future. The omniscience of the absolute spirit comprehends implicitly ás well the future as the past; therefore, can the individual by means of an intense interest of the will draw unconsciously from the unconscious knowledge of the absolute spirit as well the details of future events as particulars of the present state of the world at distant points. Inasmuch as the absolutely unconscious psychical functions of different individual souls are in the last resort only functions of the same absolute subject with relation to different organisms, from this concrete-monistic standpoint it is intelligible that the strong interest of the individual soul-will suffices to set free, irrespectively of distance, functions in the absolute subject which are directed upon the organism of another individual, and so far seem to be integrating constituents or functions of the individual soul pertaining to that organism. With the exciting or inspiring action upon the somnambulic parts of the brain of the functions thus set free, the transfer of hallucinations* to the somnambulic consciousness of others is prepared.

This explanation of both clairvoyance and transference of hallucination from far distance seems to me the only possible one, while for thought-transference in immediate proximity I hold Barrett's explanation to be true. According to him, every brain vibration corresponding to a mental representation, produces a sphere of induction-vibrations in the ether, by which similar vibrations are induced in other brains. The first half of the supposition, according to our present physical conceptions, is almost unavoidable, and it can only be doubted whether the induction-sphere is

---

* It will be observed that the word "hallucination" does not here denote mere baseless appearance, but a self-clothing of a true intuition with the form of sense, that form even often corresponding exactly, and in minutest detail, with the distant objective or future fact.—TR.

strong enough for perceptible influence upon other brains, and whether the mode of this influence is such as to induce similar representations. The facts that the parts of the brain supporting the waking consciousness are not at all, but the sensitive somnambulic parts of the brain are perceptibly influenced by thoughts of others, that the strength of this influence rapidly diminishes with distance, and is disturbed by light, seem to establish the presumption that the supposed induction-sphere of ether-vibrations is really the reason of the occurrence of a similar complex of vibrations in an adjacent brain.*

The decision is more doubtful in the case of thought-transference from a far distance, Du Prel and Hellenbach here likewise supposing a mediation by ether-vibrations. I believe, on the contrary, that this case comes under the same explanation as clairvoyance. This points to a radical communication between individuals by *rapport* or telephonic correspondence in the Absolute. I infer this from the fact that in thought-transference at a far distance no difference appears to exist between greater and lesser distances, whereas thought-transference in close proximity diminishes rapidly with remoteness (presumably in proportion to the square of the distance), thus soon reaching a limit where the influence, even with greater intensity of an individual will, ceases. It is true we see light at remote distances, yet only with an organised sense-apparatus adapted to it, and even only then if no untransparent body intervenes ; glowing balls of gigantic dimensions appearing as unextended points of faint light. If also gravitation and magnetism act through untransparent bodies, yet with diminution of force in quadratic proportion to distance, very powerful forces and correspondingly large masses are requisite for a considerable effect at remote points. The active force of

---

* This hypothesis is carried into more detail, and defended by Prof. Dr. O. Simony in his dissertation " On Spiritistic manifestations from the scientific standpoint."("Ueber spiritistische Manifestationen vom naturwissenschaflichen Standpunkt") Vienna, Hartleben, 1884.

vibrations, corresponding to an isolated thought, of limited parts of the brain, is quite incommensurately small as against the light and gravitation of the heavenly bodies. If, for example, the somnambulic consciousness were sufficiently sensitive to be affected across the ocean, or more accurately through a great part of the globe, by the induction-spheres of single detached brain-vibrations, on an ndividual so sensitive would continually stream in such a multitude of thousandfold stronger impressions, that consciousness itself would be overpowered by their mass and relative force, and life would be simply impossible. Therefore, I think that thought-transference at hand and at a distance require quite different principles of explanation, the latter having more affinity to true clairvoyance than to the former.

Accordingly it seems to me impossible to explain thought-transference at a far distance and true clairvoyance by physical mediation, and that recourse to a metaphyscial, super-sensuous explanation is unavoidable. But this supersensous explanation introduces no new hypothesis, as, for instance, that by spirits does, but rests merely on the rooting (*Urstand*) of natural individuals in the Absolute : a principle to which only Materialism can object. This explanation transcends, it is true, the mere natural sphere, but only in so far as reaching back it lays hold on the supernatural root of the given natural, without which the latter would have neither essence nor existence ; but it is not supernatural in the sense that it appeals to a sphere of existence beyond the natural, a hidden world of supernatural individuals lurking behind the given. It only declines to maintain the usual abstraction of the natural from its supernatural basis, rather considering it in its concrete unity with the latter, immanent in it as being and substance. It is just in the phenomena of true clairvoyance (*e.g.*, corpse-seeing) that no one has ever supposed the cause to lie outside the individual himself ; that is to say, the single phenomenal province which mere natural or abstract natural causes will not explain is not claimed by Spiritism.

Moreover, true clairvoyance seems not to occur with professional mediums for the sole reason that they are usually in no relations of intimacy or deep sympathy with the rest of the party, so that the interest of the will in establishing the radical connection fails. For the thought-transference in which mediums have an interest, induction of brain vibrations suffices, there being thus no need at all for the restoration of a telephonic-connection in the background ; but there is nothing to excite so deep an interest in the past and future fates of the circle and their relatives and friends, as would compel the unconscious will to draw from the absolute knowledge of its absolute basis. What the Spiritists call clairvoyance in their mediums is not that ; true clairvoyance, the tenderest, though morbid, blossom of man's unconscious spirit life, the Spiritists till now know nothing of from their mediums, because the latter carry on their business far too much as a trade. For the development of genuine clairvoyance in mediumistic circles the conditions are far more favourable when private mediums sit with their families, with lovers, and intimate friends ; if it occurs here, it may elicit the most startling revelations without driving us to any other source than those in the medium himself, and in his radical connection with his absolute basis.

In concluding this section, I cannot warn too emphatically against extending the theoretical interest, which these phenomena excite, to a practical one, or replacing the former by the latter. That the Tibetan monks have arrived at the development of thought-transference into a kind of telegraphy, implies the absence among them of a natural postal and telegraphic system. We who are in possession of such have no interest at all in accustoming ourselves to psychical actions at a distance, which yet in their hallucinatory form admit only of a very incomplete, inadequate, and uncertain mode of transmitting intelligence. Still more irrational, however, is it to cultivate the gift of clairvoyance. For if anything whatever is adapted to make life endurable, it is ignorance of the future, leaving room for hope and effort.

One who has the misfortune to foresee the deaths of his acquaintances is a mirror allowing the calamities and sufferings of the future to cast their shadows upon the present; his best success will be to keep his visions to himself, and to blunt and harden himself against the joylessness of his morbid capabilities. Since it is only important events that so far excite interest as to elicit prevision, but of the more important events of human life by far the greater part are of a sad and painful nature, it follows that prevision must anticipate far more sufferings than joys; but as these sufferings are not to be averted, the prophetic gift is in defiance of the truth that inevitable grief can never be late enough learnt. Only in quite rare exceptional cases does prevision relate to natural events (ship-wrecks, fall of houses, and the like), which threaten man with destruction if he does not withdraw himself; but such hints for avoidance of impending dangers are perhaps more rare than the gruesome irony with which prevision itself too often drives man into calamity in his attempt to escape it. Tradition is full of such instances; of the more recent I will only mention that of the engine-driver, who by moonlight saw the body of his father, as it really lay upon the rails, but angrily drove over it because on the two preceding nights at the same spot he had stopped the train in front of his hallucination for nothing. Who-ever possesses the unhappy gift of clairvoyance will do un-conditionally well to ignore it as much as possible and in no way to strengthen it by exercise, but rather to lead a sort of life not favourable to its development.

IV.

TRANSFIGURATIONS AND MATERIALISATIONS.

If a somnambule is ordered by her magnetiser to be someone else, she fulfils this command with the automaton-like will-lessness and with the hallucinatory vivacity which belong only to the somnambulic consciousness. With a slight cue she transforms herself into the figure and character of another, like an extemporising actress, expresses opinions, sympathies, antipathies, and wishes conformable to the character, and supports her talk by corresponding mimical mien and gestures, if her somnambulism is so deepened as to allow of this. The automaton-like will-lessness of somnambulism cannot be more sharply characterised, than by the readiness with which the somnambule flings off her whole personality, and adopts another diametrically opposed, perhaps, to her age, sex, character, religious belief, and political opinions. Even the human quality is given up, and exchanged for that of an animal designated by the magnetiser; the experiences of somnambulism explain the miracle of Circe naturally, supposing her magnetic force to have been strong enough to hypnotise the companions of Odysseus, and to make them see themselves and each other as swine.

What is possible in provoked somnambulism is so also in auto-somnambulism, whether the latter occurs involuntarily or is spontaneously elicited. As there are insane persons who take themselves for animals and so behave, such insane hallucinations having in former times spread epidemically (were-wolves), so also in spontaneous somnambulism of mediums can there be a self-displacement of the Ego, an inner transfiguration of the personality, manifested by corresponding demeanour, gesture, and speech. The precondition is, that the medium at passing into somnambulism fills the place of the directing magnetiser, *i.e.*, gives by the still waking will the directive for the automaton-like hallucinations. What the persons are into whom the medium, as somnambule, believes himself transfigured, will in such cases depend on the forms most engaging his phantasy, to the appearance of which, as he knows, the expectation of the spectators is directed. As mediums learn to know the tradition of Spiritist circles before they get beyond physical manifestations and thought-reading, it is explicable that certain figures are of stereotyped reproduction with quite different mediums, as Harlequin, Pierrot, Columbine, &c., in the Harlequinade ; they call themselves John King, Katie King, &c., and are supplemented by the turbaned Oriental, the pert little girl under different names, and others. With these types the phantasy of mediums has become so familiar that they at once present themselves as figures for the self-displacement of the Ego. Already in masked somnambulism they play their part when the communications, themselves maintaining more or less the character of these types, announce them as the authors of the intelligence conveyed. This persistent tradition, of course, does not prevent phantasy of different mediums conceiving figures peculiar to themselves, of which in the somnambulic state they are delivered, the somnambulic Ego—consciousness flowing over into them, no matter whether along with it an unappropriating consciousness of the persistence of the abandoned Ego asserts itself or not.

It is striking, how great a change of features, deportment, gait, &c., the somumbulic transfiguration can bring about in the external appearance of the somnambule ; the size of the figure can apparently increase or decrease, voice and utterance be quite different, and even the turgescence of the skin and the lustre (*Feuchtigkist*) of the eye can thus be changed. Even with accomplished mimics, similar changes in a degree astonishing to ordinary people are observable ; but the somnambulic transfiguration, by the vivacity and involuntary character of the hallucination, sinks the true personality in the part to be played to a degree which even the greatest dramatic genius, with all its other superiorities, cannot attain, because it still always remains conscious of its transfiguration. The deviation of the voice from the normal can go to involuntary ventriloquism, which notoriously possesses, with other peculiarities, that of altogether deceiving the ear as to the place where the voice originates. With some mediums, already in masked somnambulism different voices speak confusedly together, which announce themselves as proceeding from present but invisible spirits,* and such mediums will also support their mimical transfigurations by sprightly " speaking with tongues." Other mediums, who are not strictly " speaking mediums," confine themselves to mimical transfiguration without support by speech or with sparse addition of detached words.

It is a matter of course that a medium, who in somnambulism has dramatised the Ego into a figure of the phantasy, will involuntarily desire to be attired for the part to be played in conformity with the character assumed, so far as the means are at hand. In this irresponsible state, for instance, an otherwise modest young girl will not feel prevented from taking off her clothes and going about in shirt or chemise ; or if the hallucination is an Oriental, linen will be tied round the head for a turban. So far, however, as the available costume is not suited to the part, the medium will take care to keep behind the curtain, and to show only those parts of the body which correspond to the figure of the phantasy.

---

* [I shall never forget the storm of whoops and cries, supposed to be of "Indian spirits," which came from the little bed-room of Mrs. Huntoon's cottage at Chittenden, Vermont, just after I had thoroughly searched it, and secured the window—the only aperture, except the door before which we sat—with mosquito netting nailed outside, tested and found quite intact immediately afterwards.—TR.]

84

If the medium has the indefinite, but urgent, impulse to appear in the mimetic transfiguration, so as to fulfil the expectation of the circle, he will involuntarily seek to remove the obstructions to the satisfaction of this impulse, thus to loosen knots and strip off fastenings which the spectators have attached to him for security.

In so far as the somnambulic medium himself believes in his transformation, *i.e.*, feels himself another person, there can be no talk of intentional deception if he presents himself to the spectators as this other person ; and in case he imagines the "other person" as one deceased but surviving in the other world, he acts completely *bonâ fide* if he comes forward in the chosen costume and mimetic disguise as the apparition of a spirit from the other world. If the spectators do not understand the somnambulic state, whether they believe in the reality of a spirit apparition, or on the other hand lay hold of the "spirit" and "expose" the medium, the latter is in either case just as little to be made responsible. The medium is here just as little spirit as deceiver, but an irresponsible auto-somnambule, to be protected from fright. That there are also fraudulent representations without somnambulism is at the same time not for a moment to be disputed.

According to the best Spiritist authorities, it may be taken that in 95 per cent. of all so-called spirit-apparitions, the medium himself figures as the apparition, putting fraudulent imitations quite out of sight. It is quite vain to hope, by binding the medium to a particular place, to be secure that any apparition away from this place is not the medium ; partly because somnambules are astonishingly expert in loosening knots and stripping off fastenings, and partly because, according to Spiritist assertion, the medium can penetrate the matter of the fastenings.* Supposing

* [Of course, Spiritists do not ascribe to the conscious mediums themselves any such power, nor have they hitherto sufficiently, if at all, recognised the superior power of the somnambulic condition. It is this general unfamiliarity with the psychology of somnambulism which, in my judgment, makes the study of the author's application of it to mediumistic phenomena so important. The fact is-

this assertion to be true, it is also impossible to secure mediums by enveloping them in gauze carried round the seat and sealed, or by caging them; for if the somnambulic medium can penetrate substances, he can produce himself as an apparition notwithstanding all such precaution. . That the medium is on the seat at the beginning and close of the cabinet sitting, but meanwhile gets up, whenever a form appears (often also without such appearance), is proved by testing the weight of the chair from second to second, although these observations are not to be universally relied upon.*

This much is certain, that if the penetrability of matter by mediums is admitted, the non-identity of medium and apparition must be proved by wholly different means than by material confinement of the medium. Regard has not been had to this, even in the statement that 95 per cent. of the apparitions are substantially the medium himself, so that the 5 per cent. residue may still be much reduced. Whenever the assertion of non-identity rests on no other ground than this material confinement of the medium, it is to be rejected as utterly unproven ; everything done by the apparition is in such cases to be conceived as the act of the medium ; e.g., when it cuts off and distributes a lock of hair (Ps. St. I., 487 ; II., 22) displaces furniture, carries objects round, extends hand or arm, walks about with the spectators and converses with them, has itself photographed (II., 19-20, 22), impresses its feet, hands, or face in molten paraffin, and delivers these impressions to the spectators (VI., 526, 545-548), and so on. All such reports, intended to prove the objective reality of the apparition, are defective, because they dispose of the question of the identity of apparition and medium on the ground of the fastening or

---

that somnambulism, so far as known, has been hitherto explained among us by Spiritism (an explanation which cannot possibly survive a serious and unprejudiced examination of the facts), instead of the converse attempt being at first made, to explain mediumistic phenomena, partially at least, by somnambulism.—TR.]

* [The reference here seems to be to experiments recorded by Baron Hellenbach (" Geburt und Tod, &c." Vienna: 1885 : p. 143, et seq).—TR.]

confinement of the latter. In America, where mediums " work " in families or gangs, as it were, no value whatever is to be attached to the reports generally, since here door and gate are opened not only to somnambulic confederacy, but also to plain fraud. That hitherto all objects, flowers, samples of raiment, locks of hair, &c., delivered by such apparitions are of earthly origin, the apparitions themselves have not denied when questioned ; experts can assess the price of the material per meter quite accurately, and as to the locks of hair, it is to be observed that hair at different parts of the head varies not inconsiderably in shade and colour.

It is asserted by some Spiritists that the apparition is as a rule spatially divided from the medium, and that the latter first, when the apparition is seized, effects a junction with it by sudden penetration of the restraining material, because otherwise death would result. It seems more likely that the apparition, by dissipating itself under the hands of the seizer, and penetration of the material, should hasten back to the medium, than the reverse ; but if the medium can so suddenly penetrate the restraining material, as to reunite with the apparition in the moment of danger, one does not see why he should not rather prevent this danger, by quietly going about with and in the apparition.

There is, however, in fact, a province of phenomena, where the possibility that the apparition is the medium is excluded, and this province encroaches upon that of transfigurations of the medium, in so far as the apparition of the latter shows changes in size, form, complexion, beard, and dress, utterly unattainable by means at the service of the medium in the cabinet. When before the sitting the medium is closely searched, has even exchanged his own clothes for others of easily recognisable cut and colour, the locality being under strict control, it is not to be seen whence the medium should get the means of disguise, how he should provide himself with white gauzy raiment, stout material

with heavy draperies, beards, turbans, masks, buskins, &c.
If, nevertheless, the spectators see him appear as figures of
different age, sex, size, clothing, nationality, &c., other
causes of this phenomenon must be sought for.

What may help us on the right road, is first the circumstance, that such uncommon and apparently inexplicable
phenomena seldom or never appear to spectators present
for the first time at a mediumistic sitting, and that even
frequenters must with a new medium go through many
sittings where only physical phenomena occur, until the
medium's own somnambulic consciousness announces that
the time is come for attempting transfigurations. It is an
universal experience that phenomena are more plentiful
and extraordinary, the more sittings the medium has held
with the same circle, and that every newly introduced
member interrupts or quite arrests progress. It follows
that close *rapport* between medium and participators must
be established, before transfigurations and materialisations
can succeed, and that depends, not on mere human,
friendly, relations between their waking consciousnesses, but
only on a relation between their somnambulic consciousnesses, *i.e.*, on a magnetic *rapport*.

The physical phenomena progress in proportion as the
participators are trained to be unconscious auxiliary
mediums, as they learn, that is, to give off more and more
nerve force, and to make over this to the disposal of the
medium ; the ideality of the manifestations is the more
astonishing, the more they expose themselves to the
medium's will to thought-reading, suffer to be implanted
in them the unconscious will to thought-transference to the
medium, and let themselves be stimulated by the medium
to the development of a masked somnambulic consciousness of the hyperæsthetic somnambulic memory. When
their latent mediumship has been thus in some degree
awakened, and the magnetic power of the unconscious will
of the medium over their masked somnambulic conscious-

ness is sufficiently established, the medium, whose somnambulic consciousness is very sensible of this concurrence of auxiliary mediums, can pass on to phenomena which presuppose a certain power over the souls of the spectators.

With different members of a small circle, the power obtained by the medium in the course of preceding sittings will be different; consequently the amount of phenomena confirmed by different spectators must be different. This fact is seldom enough regarded ; instead of each spectator giving his own report, without consultation with the rest, of every sitting, the party agree upon a common account, in which the subjective diversity of the phenomena disappears. Whereas it is easy to agree upon the physical phenomena (except lights), with transfigurations and materialisations it is often quite otherwise, especially on their first appearance ; afterwards, when all the party have fallen sufficiently under the power of the medium, in this province also the testimonies will be again more consentient.

At first the medium usually only puts out for a few moments before the curtain single parts of the body, hands, arms, head; gradually showing the whole upper body or quite emerging. Then at once it appears that some of the spectators think they recognise the medium without a doubt, and see nothing else whatever than his form, while others, with a sort of mutual agreement, declare the apparition to have been essentially different from the medium. Similarly at table-sittings in the light, individuals present have seen different shaped hands come from under the table, at a considerable distance from the medium, whose hands lay visible to all upon the table, while the others have seen nothing whatever of this. Evidently, in such cases there is a transfer of the medium's hallucinations into the somnambulic consciousnesses of the sufficiently sensitive of the party, for we have seen already how favourable to hallucination-transference the relations in such a situation are.

With us Westerns, consciously or unconsciously-willed

hallucination-transference to a recipient in waking consciousness, who has not the will to be hallucinated, and does not at all suspect that the figure perceived by him is the transferred hallucination of a third person, is something extremely uncommon. But the history of religious excitements affords a number of examples of whole assemblies of ecstatics infected as much by hallucinations as by convulsions and Vitus-dance, when, it is true, speech powerfully assists in giving definite direction to the phantasies of the recipients. Examples of this kind are, moreover, to be found in all those cases where living or dying waking or dreaming persons transport themselves with ardent longing and hallucinatory vividness into the proximity of another at a distance, and produce in the latter, by the *rapport* thus restored, a corresponding hallucination of their personal presence. (*Ps. St.* VI., 294, 344 ; VII., 47, *et seq.*) Here it is to be remarked, first, that the success of the experiment with sufficiently sensitive recipients seems not dependent upon knowledge of their locality for the time being, so that thought can be directed to it, and second, that if generally the environment of the recipient is represented in both consciousnesses, its perspective still appears different in each, according to the actual or supposed position in it of the seer. Transference in Europe seems seldom to have extended to other hallucinations than the personal apparitions of the transferor; only in "second-sight" or true clairvoyance infection of hallucinations by the true seer to predisposed companions appears to occur.*

On the other hand, cases of hallucination-transference

---

* See *Ps. St.* IX., 152-154, for a very evident case of this. The instance adduced by Schopenhauer (Parerga, 2nd Ed., I., 316-317) is quite simply explained by the fact that the imprisoned medium had the hallucination, which he transferred to the fellow-prisoners who had fallen under his magnetic influenc e, twice in sleep and only on the third occasion when awake, so that the agreeme n t of the apparition seen by the others on the two first occasions with the simu ltaneous dream image of the sleeping medium could not be tested. It is highly probable that animal ₂ are also susceptible to the transference of hallucinations (comp. Owen : " T he Debateable Land " ; " Davis : " The Magic Staff ") ; and, indeed, it would not be surprising if with the relative preponderance of the middle brain in animals their average susceptibility to this should be greater than that of human beings.

are more frequently reported of Indian fakirs and Turkish dervishes. One is made, for instance, to see a coil of poisonous snakes beneath a raised cloth, where immediately afterwards nothing is visible (*Ps. St.* IV., 200); or in a closed room is seen at one time a flock of wild geese flying; at another a number of snakes curling about; at another the walls drawing together as if they were about to crush one. (IX., 469, 470.*)

Recently magnetisers have produced the phenomenon of transference of hallucinations even in public representations, but have first placed the recipients in the hypnotic state, and, moreover, made use of the word of command in order to educe the hallucination. They have thus caused a substance with a nasty taste to be eaten for one with a pleasant taste, a stick to be seen as a snake, and excited the belief that the magnetiser was floating about in the air (*Ps. St.* III., 536, 537), and so on. What with the help of speech a magnetiser awake can do with a perfect stranger in open somnambulism is possible without speech to a somnambulic magnetiser with a masked somnambule who is better known to him; what in the above-mentioned instance is possible with sensitive recipients at a far distance, is possible with non-sensitive recipients in proximity. If the urgent wish of the somnambulic transferor is not to transfer his hallucination of his personal presence to a distant recipient, but is rather directed to transfer to a recipient close by his hallucination of the personal presence of deceased spirits, there will be a corresponding change of the recipient's perception. If, for instance, the medium has the hallucination that he is no longer himself, but, say, the spirit of John King or Katie King, the hallucination will pass to the recipient that the medium stepping in front of the curtain is no longer the medium but John King or Katie King. If, in another case, the medium has the illusion that from the pit of his stomach a mist develops, and

---

* [See "LIGHT," September 9th, 1882, for a translation of this case.—TR.]

out of the mist a spirit form, the fascinated spectator will likewise have the same hallucination. (IX., 83; IV., 546-548.)

Psychiatry distinguishes between hallucinations in the narrower sense, and illusions, understanding by the former a product of the phantasy without a foundation of sense-perception, by the latter phantastic transformations of sense-perceptions. So that it is an hallucination if a coiled-up snake is seen lying on a plate, but an illusion if a stick or rope is taken for a snake; an hallucination, if a misty form is seen growing out of a medium, but an illusion, if the medium himself is seen as the apparition of a spirit. Moreover, the boundary is fluid, hallucination and illusion passing into one another, for apart from conditions in which sense-perception is closed, every hallucination must dispossess a segment of sense-perception, and introduce itself among the momentary collective sense-perceptions, and on the other hand there are illusions in which trans-formation of the completely contrary sense-perception at their foundation seem to be more difficult than would be an original construction on a neutral ground. Thus illu-sions and hallucinations pass into one another when at one time the medium himself is regarded as a wholly different figure; at another an apparition very like the medium is mistaken for the latter; or lastly, medium and phantom are seen to separate and come together again. With slight deviations of the form from the medium (as in Crookes' observations) hallucination-transference is evi-dently facilitated by the medium coming forward; when the deviations are great, hallucination may be easier to implant than illusion.

Ordinarily, perception of the same phenomenon by several observers is sufficient guarantee of its objectivity; but this is no longer the case when the relations are exceptionally favourable to hallucination-transference. For although here also identity of the transcendent cause may be concluded from agreement of the effect, yet this identical cause is not here a material thing (in itself) in real objective space, affecting the senses of those present, but the subjective hallucination of the medium, affecting the somnambulic consciousnesses by induction of similar brain vibrations. In these cases, therefore, we have to look for other marks of distinction between perception and hallucination.

When a form is seen, with opportunity of contact, and the hand passes through without resistance, the probability that there is here a bare vision, or hallucination of sight, will doubtless be very great, but this is no certainty, for there are bodily forms of matter in such conditions of aggregation that their surfaces reflect light, but are not perceptible by touch. It seems to be a sure test of the objectivity of forms, known to be different from the medium by observing them originate and disappear, that they cast a shadow, are reflected in a mirror (Owen), appear magnified or reduced when seen through magnifying or diminishing glasses, and are duplicated by a prism. Nevertheless, this would be a fallacious conclusion, for hallucinations have all these properties also ; indeed, the magnifying and diminishing through glasses, and the duplication through a prism is made use of in psychiatry, like distention and contraction of the pupils on approximation and removal of the form, as a test to distinguish genuine hallucinations from mere representations of the phantasy, or feigned hallucinations. Photography alone can afford a safe proof of the hallucinatory character of a seen form, when plates of sufficient sensitiveness for the apparent light-strength of the apparition show no chemical impression. With self-luminous phenomena, usually, as already remarked, the super-frangible rays so predominate, that the plate shows impressions even when non-sensitive observers see nothing at all ; but with phenomena not possessing self-illuminating power, momentarily flashing electric curve-lamps, or burning magnesium wire, will give a sudden illumination sufficient to secure positive results in case of the objectivity of the phenomenon.

In fact, all photographic experiments hitherto attempted with forms which were seen by the spectators tell against the objectivity of the phenomena, for in all cases hitherto reported there were no results except when the medium himself was admitted into the photograph. In the latter cases the pictures are not distinct enough for it to be decided whether, besides the form of the medium, the illusion disguising him has also attained to photographic reproduction; in other words, whether the photograph obtained resembles the phantom, and not merely the medium inherent in it. The photograph taken by Crookes, on which is to be seen the medium simultaneously with the phantom, is exposed to the strong suspicion that instead of the supposed phantom the medium, and instead of the supposed medium the dress of the medium, stuffed with a cushion in a half-concealed position, have been photographed. Since material restraint of the medium affords no security, a simultaneous taking of medium and phantom would have to be shown, before objectivity could be conceded to apparitions perceived merely by the sight of the spectators.* All photographs hitherto produced, which seem to fulfil this condition, have turned out to be either the fraud of speculative photographers (*Ps. St.* II., 338, 345), or are much open to the suspicion of having been deceptively manufactured by too zealous Spiritists for the conversion of unbelievers.†

* [Dr. von Hartmann will, I am sure, not object to a quotation here from Mr. Crookes, that readers may appreciate the extent to which collective hallucination must be supposed to go, if only the photographic test above required is sufficient to exclude that possibility. "During the photographic séances, Katie" (the spirit) "muffled her medium's head up in a shawl to prevent the light falling upon her face. I frequently drew the curtain on one side while Katie was standing near, and it was a common thing for the seven or eight of us in the laboratory to see Miss Cook" (the medium) "and Katie at the same time, under the full blaze of the electric light. We did not on these occasions see the face of the medium because of the shawl, *but we saw her hands and feet; we saw her move uneasily under the influence of the intense light, and we heard her moan occasionally.* I have one photograph of the two together, but Katie is seated in front of Miss Cook's head." (Italics mine.)—Crookes' "Phenomena of Spiritualism" (Burns, 1874), p. 109.—Tr.]
† The translator is unaware of any evidence of the *latter* suggestion.

Ordinarily, detection of a possible deception of one sense is sought by help of the other senses, the agreement of several being considered sufficient guarantee of objectivity. This is quite enough, when the question is of particular sense-deceptions in waking consciousness, but not when it is of actual hallucinations, *i.e.*, transferences from the somnambulic into the waking consciousness; for here the number of the senses sharing the hallucination rises with the vivacity of the latter. The weakest degree of hallucination concerns only a single sense, either that of touch alone (contacts by invisible hands), or of hearing alone (storm-bells, fire-bells, music of the spheres, war-alarums, human voices), or of smell alone (characteristic scent of a person or locality), or of sight alone. With increasing energy of the somnambulic consciousness, hallucination of one sense evokes the feelings and perceptions naturally associated with it of the other senses, when the accessory feeling elicited may enter consciousness even before the principal hallucination, should the dramatic course of the whole hallucination so require it. For instance, one first hears the outer door unlocked, opened, and closed, then steps in the hall, then the room door open, and then first occurs vision, while in less vivid cases the accompanying and preceding hallucination of hearing is absent, and the room door seems to open without sound, if the form does not enter through the closed door. The vision now approaching the observer, if the latter recognises in it an acquaintance, the hallucination of the smell of scent commonly used by the acquaintance may very easily associate itself, and finally, the figure may lay a hand upon his shoulder, the hallucination of touch being then associated. These combined hallucinations of four senses will, however, not afford the least guarantee for the objectivity of the apparition ; rather will the well-founded presumption, that *one* of these different feelings of sense is hallucinatory, suffice as foundation for the suspicion that they are all so, and originate from a common hallucinatory source.

Applying these principles to mediumistic phenomena, from the well-founded presumption of the hallucinatory constitution of visible phantoms, we have to derive the suspicion that feelings of touch also, associated with these visions, or alternating with them, are mere hallucinations. It is true we must here be on our guard against over-hasty generalisation, as is already shown by the circumstance that hitherto hallucinations of hearing do not seem to have been observed at mediumistic sittings, the voices heard being rather the somnambulically feigned voice of the medium. Only if it is true that several voices appear to come from different parts of the room, not only in quick alternation, but sometimes also in the strict sense of the word to intermingle speech simultaneously : only then would it be necessary to speak of mediumistic hallucinations of hearing.

As to hallucinations of touch in particular, the possibility remains that felt pressure of invisible or visionary hands, feet, &c., is also derived from a system of dynamical push-and-pull lines, presenting the analogy of the pressure of hand-surfaces without corporeity behind them, just as impressions of this sort may be supposed to arise. Whether in the particular case there is a dynamical influence of mediumistic nerve force, or only a transferred hallucination, is not to be determined from the simultaneous visibility or invisibility of the supposed hand ; for as a dream can create in itself the suitable sense-perceptions, so also may the vision of a hand be fused for consciousness with a really perceived hand-pressure (without hand) into the unity of an apparent object of perception, just as well as hallucinations of sight and touch of the hand might be fused for the unity of an apparent object of perception. This fusion for the unity of an apparent object belongs even to the content of the hallucination to be transferred,

H

in so far as the medium's own somnambulic consciousness has already accomplished this fusion ; and indeed it is then quite indifferent, whether the medium has fused the visual hallucination of the hand with the phantasy image of the tactile hallucination to be produced, or with the phantasy image of the tactile perception to be produced by his mediumistic nerve force.

Should the part of the observer's body which is supposed to be pressed be undoubtedly outside the medium's range of action, it is certain that one has only to do with combined hallucinations of sight and touch ; in other cases there remains a doubt, which can only be decided in favour of a combination of visual hallucination with real impressions of mediumistic nerve force, if the same supposed hand or foot, without interruption of its visibility, immediately afterwards effects a permanent impression on a suitable material. This experiment, so far as I am aware, has never been made ; I know of only one isolated report, that in a materialisation sitting an impression of a simultaneously visible (but not palpable) child's foot was produced (*Ps. St.* VII., 397), and this when the curtain, behind which the medium sat, was raised, thus undoubtedly within the medium's range of action.*

This report requires, first, confirmation by similar observations of others ; yet it receives some support from various instances, weakly attested it is true, which are said to have spontaneously occurred outside mediumistic sittings.

Someone, for example, is reminded of a person by seeing, in a half-somnambulistic state, a hand near him write the name of the person in question ; or a ship is caused to alter its course, and to save a wrecked vessel by the steersman seeing in the cabin the captain of a strange ship sitting and writing, the words " steer to the west " ·

---

* [*Wirkungsphare.* The "action" here referred to is that of the mediumistic nerve force. There is no suggestion of ordinary physical action.—TR.]

being thereupon found in the ship's book in a strange writing. Should the view not be preferred, that the writing was produced unconsciously, and without subsequent recollection, by the hands of observers themselves in the somnambulic state, there remains only the assumption that they were spontaneous writing mediums, with the capacity for writing at a distance, and that in this way, thus themselves writing at a distance, they brought to consciousness ideas transferred to them from a distance, or resulting from their clairvoyance, while at the same time they had the vision of a strange hand or person writing. It would not be surprising, if in the case of writing at a distance by mediums also,* it should thereupon be reported that the strange writing hand had been seen by the observers, which up to the present has not happened, so far as I am aware, at least not at sittings in the light ; but that would not afford the least ground for seeking in such visible hand anything else than a transferred hallucination of sight.

The case is similar, when seen forms, as to which there is a certainty that they are pure hallucinations and not mere illusions, raise material objects, carry them about, hand them to a spectator, take them back, and restore them to their places. All this may form part of the transferred hallucinations, as well as the approximation of the walls of the room in the example above mentioned ; but it can be proved by the changed positions of particular objects after the sitting that there has been actually an objective displacement of material things. When these movements have happened within the range of action of the medium's nerve force, and do not exceed the mode and strength of performances by means of this force, there is no reason for referring them to any other cause. The somnambulic medium has then fused his hallucination of the presented forms with the figuration by phantasy of the displacements

---

* [*i.e.,* at séances.—TR.]

of objects, has unconsciously effected the latter by his mediumistic nerve force, having himself the honest belief that the forms of his phantasy have effected these displacements by their own power ; by transference of his hallucination to the spectators he has then also at the same time transferred to them the involuntary conviction that the seen displacements of things are effected by the hallucinated forms.

Further, I know no report of such movements of material things by phantoms, from which it appears that the reporters had been aware of the necessity and difficulty of distinguishing between hallucinations and illusions ; all reports of this sort up to the present suggest the supposition that the supposed exhibitions of the force by the forms were simply muscular performances by the mediums, who were resident in (*drinsteckten*) the phantom.

When an apparition tears off its veil pieces which dissolve like cobwebs between the fingers of the spectator, and when it thereupon repairs the holes in the veil by shaking it out, it is clear that this is a case of combined hallucinations of sight and touch. When, on the other hand, the figure lets the spectator cut off pieces from its garment, which feel stout, like earthly material, a doubt arises whether there is here hallucination of touch, or an *apport* of a real object. If the samples, likewise, afterwards dissolve, or are not to be found after the sitting, their hallucinatory character is to be considered proved ; if they afterwards exist, and can be priced per piece, their reality, and at the same time their earthly derivation are indubitable. When a figure standing within the range of the medium's action, wears a piece of earthly material, there remains the possibility that the medium, by his nerve force, keeps this material suspended and approaches it to the spectator, and by the same force applies scissors for the cutting, all in hallucinatory projection upon the visionary form, which need not for all that have, itself, the least reality. More obviously suggested, certainly, is the suspicion that a form wearing earthly material and cutting pieces from it with scissors is no hallucination, but an illusion superinduced upon the medium, who is the agent. Just because this form is illusory, that is, bears in itself a number of hallucinatory elements, can it also wear hallucinatory attire (veil, &c.), which for touch appears as dissolving cobweb, or impalpable nothing.

It will be for future materialisation-sittings, above all, to distinguish, first, whether the forms seen are illusions or hallucinations; secondly, whether in the latter case their supposed actions leave behind durable effects which can be exhibited; and, thirdly, whether such effects have been accomplished within or external to the range of action of the medium's nerve force. That a form is a pure hallucination, and not an illusion, is only to be established by the test, that either the hand grasps through it, or its origination or disappearance is observed (*Ps. St.* VI., 292; IX., 146, 147), or it is seen at the same time with the somnambulic medium, when confederacy is unquestionably excluded (VIII., 435; IX., 157; Hellenbach's "Geburt und Tod," 114). These proofs failing, there is always only to be admitted an illusion which includes the medium, because this case is the common one, and the pure hallucination of detached phantoms is the rare exception. At all events, it is once more to be remembered that this proximate supposition is not excluded when the medium is bound or confined in a cage.

Existing reports from Spiritist circles up to now seem to me to contain no statements whatever which could necessitate our going beyond the proximate explanation by hallucination-transference, in combination with the action at a distance of mediumistic nerve force. Nothing has ever been reported of durable mechanical effects by pure phantoms, detached, that is, from the medium, beyond the range of the latter's nerve force. So long as this is not the case, it seems to me scientifically unwarranted to attribute objective reality to the alleged subjective apparitions, and to devise hypotheses for the explanation of them as objectively real apparitions. Experiments for determining alteration of weight of the medium during the appearance of the apparitions, and the weight of the apparitions themselves by their stepping on a weighing machine, seem well adapted to bring this question to a decision, if by a self-registering apparatus the possibility was excluded of hallucinatory reading off during the sitting ; but against this is the circumstance, that in consequence of charging with mediumistic nerve force, the medium himself, even without giving off matter to the apparition, may considerably diminish his weight, and may in the same way dynamically weight the machine while the apparition appears to be upon it, also without the apparition itself possessing reality and weight. Thus, by this means nothing can be established with certainty.*

Further, even supposing the Spiritists to be right in assuming that the medium gives off part of his organic matter, and thereout constructs a form of materiality which gradually increases in density, still would not only the whole matter of this objectively real apparition thus be derived from the bodily organism of the medium, but also its form from the somnambulic phantasy of the medium, and the dynamical effects possibly developed by it from the nerve force of the medium ; it would be, do, and effect nothing than what the somnambulic phantasy of the medium prescribed to it and realised by means of the forces and substances of his organism at its disposal. Even in this case no pretext would be given for recourse to another cause than the medium, as has been comprehensively and convincingly shown by Janisch.† Meanwhile, until quite different proof is adduced than hitherto, the term

---

* In the single case known to me where an apparition was weighed its weight agreed with that of the medium (*Ps. St.*VIII., 52), from which is to be concluded that it was the medium himself who stepped upon the scale.

"materialisation " must be decidedly rejected as misleading
and unwarranted ; the phantoms of so-called materialisation-
sittings are, after all which can be said of them up to the
present, really only phantoms, *i.e.*, subjective phenomena
without objective reality, but phenomena, the relative
agreement of which in the spectators is explained by their
origin in the somnambulic medium's hallucination, transferred to the spectators.

V.

THE SPIRIT HYPOTHESIS.

We have now run through the whole province of
phenomena heretofore observed in mediumistic sittings,
and can very easily understand how by these in part
highly astonishing phenomena the belief in spirits as their
causes can be excited in those who, without comprehensive
survey and careful criticism, give themselves up to the
immediate impression of their experiences. Add belief in
the existence of bodiless spirits and in the possibility of
their manifestation ; further, the yearning for restoration of
the intercourse, interrupted by death, with beloved relatives
and friends, and that they fall at length under the fascinating influence of mediums, and of the hallucinations transferred from the latter to themselves, and it would be really
psychologically inexplicable if they escaped referring part
of the phenomena to supernatural causes beyond the
mediums. On the other hand, we have seen that, for unprejudiced critical judgment in the province traversed, with
exception of true clairvoyance, there is not the slightest
occasion to overstep natural explanations, and that the

---

† "Gedanken üher Geister-materialisation," by Dr. Janisch, Real-schuldi-
rector. (*Ps. St.* VII., 115-122, 177-184, 207-213.)

appearance of the contrary rests upon a psychologically explicable, but scientifically indefensible, deception. The untenability of the Spiritistic explanation will be still better apparent if we trace its gradual spiritualisation in the course of time from the grossest sensuousness, by which, however, it has also more and more cut the ground from under its feet, to the small foot-breadth whereon it now artificially balances itself, without being able from this unstable position to contribute any real explanation.

The simple, sensuous, naïve, popular belief is that the deceased survive in their old forms, but with a shadowy, penetrable, imponderable, invisible body, and wander sadly about for a long time in their wonted localities before resolving on a thorough departure from this earth, and ascent to heavenly or descent into infernal regions, from which they can then only exceptionally and transitorily return. These spirits it is, who, attracted in some inexplicable way by the proximity of a medium, manifest their presence by rappings, pushing about furniture, table movements, writing without contact, voices, and so on, and at length by borrowing vital force (blood) from the medium can become visible in their proper forms. When an explanation of something is wanted, a spirit must have done it; how the spirit has brought the phenomenon about is his affair; a spirit must be able to do everything, just because he is a spirit. This belief, common to all the old nations and in the main also still to the lower populace of to-day, has received its systematic development among the Indians, who suppose that besides the Pitris (ancestor-spirits) living persons also leave their bodies, and with their immortal astral body or phantom can transport themselves to distant places to appear to others. A psychology which is not yet better acquainted with the province of hallucinations must necessarily grasp at such an hypothesis; we however, may be content to estimate the latter according to this its historical and psychological foundation.

This naïve belief in spirits receives in application to mediumistic phenomena its first blow from the considera tion, that the medium in that case is also a spirit, and that if in the somnambulic state he has freed himself from the limitations of the ordinary body, he must also be able to do all that spirits of the deceased could do. It could thus be conceived that the spirit of the medium has gone out with his astral body from his entranced body, moves about in the room, and makes a disturbance with the other spirits that are present. Here then already is a division of labour between the spirits and the spirit of the medium, but the way in which the medium's own spirit performs its part is still the same crassly sensuous one, as that in which the ancestor-spirits also act, namely, by contact of the limbs of their invisible astral body, to the exclusion of all mechanical action at a distance. So the explanation by spirits appeared still always as the proximate one, that through the vagrant spirit of the medium as one derivative, and immediately involved in difficulties if the medium was not in cataleptic hypnosis but in waking or masked somnambulic consciousness.

The idea once conceived, that some of the phenomena proceed from the medium himself, now demands its rights for the case also of his continuing conscious, and the demonstration of mediumistic nerve-force and its effects at a certain distance subverts the naïve conception. The mediumistic nerve-force was designated by the misleading term "psychic force," and its seat was therefore sought in the soul instead of in the nervous system of the medium. The explanation of the phenomena by the psychic force of the medium was now all at once accepted as the proximate one, and the assistance of the psychic force of spirits as derivative. For a very slight critical circumspection must lead to the perception, that spirits having invisible, impalpable astral limbs, penetrative of all matter, and without muscles and bones, could also not lay hold and raise, but must accomplish their dynamical effects in a spiritual way, for which the "psychical force" of the medium seemed to offer the closest and only analogy.

With the attainment of this reversed position, it followed that the trial must next be made, how far explanation of the phenomena by referring them to the medium sufficed, recourse to that by spirits being then first allowable, if the former explanation should appear for any reason defective. Already at this point, probably, would the spirit hypothesis have collapsed, if only the physical phenomena had had to be dealt with ; but so long as the co-operation of spirits appeared still indispensable, at any rate, for the ideality of the manifestations and for the supposed materialisations, there was no hesitation in admitting the co-operation of the re-affirmed spirits also in the physical phenomena. But already in this phase it began to be confessed that most of the phenomena were to be referred to the medium as their single cause. Davis (" Present Age," pp. 197, 161, 134) had already admitted this of 60 per cent. of the phenomena, and the later German Spiritists, like Hellenbach, carry this admission much further still.

Just for closer occupation with the materialisation phenomena was it reserved yet further to undermine the spirit-hypothesis. As long as people were involved in the naïve belief the spirits managed all the rappings and table movements with their own hands, and spoke without making use of the medium's organs of speech, the co-operation of the medium in materialisations remained limited to suffering the substances of his body to be drawn off by the spirits, who used them to make their forms wandering invisibly among us, visible and palpable. The external ordering of sittings was guided by this idea, and no Spiritist at first thought that the medium could be actively participant in the affair. This naïve conception was shattered by numerous "exposures," in which the captured phantom was unmasked as the medium himself. Now first began the distinction between transfigurations and materialisations, and finally the abidance of the produced phantom with the medium had to be recognised as the rule, and its detachment as the exception. Moreover, the detachment remained usually incomplete ; sometimes only limbs or heads, or mere trunk with stumps (*Ps. St.* VIII. 53 ; IX., 146-147) were visible at some distance from the medium ; sometimes from the lower part of the recumbent medium's body there rose over the upper part the upper part of a phantom. When, however, a complete detachment ensued, and the phantom was observed in the process of its origination and disappearance, it appeared that it streamed out wholly and entirely from the medium, and streamed back into him, and that not as a prepared form gradually filling itself with and again emptying itself of substance, out as a formless cloud, first gradually acquiring shape, and again dissolving into shapelessness.

It thence undoubtedly followed that the *medium himself* was the unconscious producer of the phantoms, as well of those detached as of those undetached, that in the medium was to be sought, not only the passive source of substance for the visibility of the forms, but besides the substance-giving also the form-giving and *formative cause* of the apparitions, of the objective reality of which no doubt at first arose in the Spiritist camp. It then needed very little critical reflection to see that spirits, whether thought of as free from body altogether or clothed with an astral body, ether body, or meta organism, must in any case belong to a wholly different order of things, and that in no case did they go about among us invisibly with a form of the same spatial dimensions as the organisms they laid aside at death, least of all clothed with spiritual garments, like those worn in life, so that there could be no talk of a mere making visible of the already present form. If a spirit would be manifest to spectators, it is easy to conceive that he would choose for this purpose the form and clothing known to them from his former life, but this form must first be completely reproduced, and to that the spirit as such would be unequal, and must require the substance-giving and form-giving production of the medium. To the spirit, if he wishes to manifest to us, there is nothing for it but to enter the medium, and with the substances and forces of the latter thence to make himself recognisable, like one who is stuck in a sack, and can only gesticulate through it.

Thus Spiritism arrived at regarding all physical effects and all materialisation phenomena as products of the medium, and at considering the spirits only as the machine-masters, whose will and intelligence stand behind the mediums in the intention to manifest, and set going the powers hidden in the organism. The spirits according to this view have ceased immediately and personally to bring about effects in the realm of earthly nature, but remain the transcendent causes of the phenomena which the medium produces without will and consciousness. A critical solution of the confusion of "mediumistic nerve-force" with "psychical force" must necessitate the abandonment of the simple sense belief in spirits; for whatever else spirits may have in themselves, a nervous system by means of which they could produce discharges of nerve-force (as roaches electrical discharges), they have as little as a muscular system, by means of which they would lift and shove tables and chairs.

Thus the hypothesis of the direct agency of spirits is refined to that of spirit agency exclusively mediated by the medium; the latter is now the only executive, and the spirits retire to the position of mere intellectual authors of the phenomena. Since, however, they take possession of the will-less and consciousless medium, the psychical side of the production is still reserved to them, and it is for the present only the bodily side which they have had to resign to the medium. The spirit of the medium himself is thereby, so far as necessary, temporarily dispossessed of its governance over the body, and its place is assumed by the "controlling spirit." It is therefore the will of the controlling spirit which so directs and guides the innervation-impulse proceeding from the medium's brain that involuntary muscular movements arise in the medium's limbs, or mediumistic nerve-force is developed; it is the strange spirit in person who through the corpse of the medium produces manuscript or writing at a distance. Just so is it this spirit, whose phantasy broods over the form to be materialised, and which effectuates the forces laid up and slumbering in the medium's organism. The whole external side of the phenomena has now its origin in the medium, and only the inner side, the ideal content of the manifestations, is it now, which seems to make co-operation of spirits indispensable, and that because it is presupposed that the medium in the consciousless sleep-state has no longer intelligence for the disposition of the phenomena, and in the waking state has no other than the waking consciousness which is unparticipant in them.

The hypothesis of mediate spirit agency may at this stage be called the *hypothesis of possession*; for so far as his true consciousness has lost dominion over his organism, the medium is possessed by the controlling spirits. In this proceeding the spirit of the medium is entirely thrown off. Either he is sunk in complete unconsciousness, or the remnant of persisting consciousness no longer commands the innervation-impulse requisite to the occurrence of the phenomena, has even no direct knowledge of the use which the controlling spirit makes of his organism and its forces, but just like the spectators is first aware of the phenomena when they have occurred, and have become perceptible to sense. This hypothesis of possession is, of course, a great advance upon the simple spirit-belief, because it takes into account observed facts, at least in relation to the external side of the phenomena, but it is untenable, because it still does not take them into account in relation to the inner side, *i.e.*, the ideality of the manifestations. It corresponds to a psychology which by the human spirit understands nothing but the contents of its normal, waking consciousness, and has still no suspicion of relatively or absolutely unconscious desires, feelings, and ideas. It is utterly confuted by the single fact of somnambulism, that there is a condition in which people give expression to the content of their consciousness by words and acts while their waking consciousness is quite suppressed or debilitated, and in which the (subsequent or simultaneous) waking consciousness knows nothing of the contents of the somnambulic consciousness, while the latter is nevertheless aware of the former. If a medium in somnambulic consciousness can by word of mouth accurately disclose the purport of a previously produced writing at a distance, of which his waking consciousness knew nothing, this affords cogent proof that the somnambulic consciousness of the medium is not thrown off or overleaped in his mediumistic results, but is somehow participant in them. This is proved by the fact that all manifestations show a content corresponding to the medium's intellectual level and ideas, that they are all coloured by the local and personal tone, so to speak, of the medium. Advancing from the explanation of transfiguration and materialisation phenomena by dynamical substantial efflorescence from the medium to that by hallucination-transference, hallucination in the medium's somnambulic consciousness (in connection with the will to transfer) has thus attained increased importance as the immediate origin of the subjective phenomena of the spectators.

Now if the participation of the somnambulic consciousness, together with the action of the parts of the brain supporting it, must undeniably be admitted, it follows that the passage of the controlling spirit's ideas and volitions can no longer be thought of as a purely passive proceeding; on the other hand the co-operation of the controlling spirit with the medium's spirit cannot be conceived as a concurrence in the control over the organism, such as actually exists between the somnambulic and waking consciousness in masked somnambulism. Rather must the single dominion over those parts and forces of the organism, which the mediumistic phenomena bring into play, be conceded to the somnambulic consciousness and the parts of the brain supporting it; and the agency of the controlling spirit must be confined to eliciting in the somnambulic consciousness of the medium those desires, feelings, and ideas, which are requisite for the spirit manifestation. Then away goes utterly the conception of possession, for it is converted into the heterogeneous conception of inspiration; the hypothesis of possession has become refined throughout into the *hypothesis of inspiration*.

According to the inspiration-hypothesis, it is the medium's own somnambulic consciousness which will write particular sentences or bring about the apparition of a particular form; but what sentences and what form hovers before it for production shall not depend on psychical processes in the medium's spirit, but upon what thoughts or form the controlling spirit conveys from its consciousness into the somnambulic consciousness of the medium. Now first is the intellectual authorship of spirits reduced to its true and finer sense, because demanding as its correlate not simply a temporarily lifeless organism but the unity of body and soul of the executive person. First at this turn the spirit-hypothesis enters a stage which enables psychology and metaphysics becomingly to deal with it seriously and critically, whereas the foregoing is to serve only for the historical information of the reader.

Thought-transference is a conception already current with us; if there are "spirits" it could well be supposed possible from a spirit to a man, as it is possible between two men. Meanwhile there are still difficulties in this supposition which are not to be under-rated. The spirit of a deceased person has no brain, whose vibrations could induce similar vibrations in a human brain in proximity ; mechanical mediation by ether vibrations, as we can suppose them in thought-transference between persons in immediate proximity without contact, thus fails for spirits who would transmit, and there only remains the other kind of thought-transference without material mediation, which seems to be limited to no distance. In fact, also, later Spiritists suppose on the ground of mediumistic communications (*kungebungen*) that the controlling spirit may be at any distance whatever from the manifesting medium, without the intimacy of the *rapport* between them being thereby prejudiced. The misfortune here only is that at far distances, according to our experiences, no thoughts or words whatever can be transferred, but only sensible and most lively hallucinations, such as seem exclusively able to be developed in the parts of the brain supporting somnambulic consciousness ; but spirits have no brains, neither the parts supporting waking, nor those supporting somnambulic consciousness, and their thoughts can, therefore, hardly be conscious with that lively hallucinatory sensuousness, rendered possible only by the somnambulic parts of the brain, which are proximate to the sense apparatus. There is no sort of pretext for admitting that the conditions of thought-transference from a spirit to the somnambulic consciousness of a man are more favourable than for that from the somnambulic consciousness of another man ; there is nothing apparent which could compensate for the difficulty suggested, so that one has to fall back on the naïve popular belief that a spirit must be able to do everything just because he is a spirit. Just that, for instance, which is characteristic of the effective representation of a deceased person in the phantasy of a medium at a materialisation sitting, the hallucinatory sensuousness, must be wanting to the self-representation of the spirit, while that with which one could soonest credit the spirit, the wordless ideal substance of sentences to be written, is again, according to our experiences, not transferable at a distance.

To these formal difficulties of transference are added others still, relating to the purport of the communications. This purport is usually *below* the intellectual level of the medium and those present, and at the highest comes *up* to it, but is never *above* it. The fact is quite intelligible, if the somnambulic consciousness of the medium is the sole intellectual source, but it demolishes the spirit hypothesis. For if the spirits have, or from the position of things are able to reveal, nothing better than what we ourselves already know, away goes the single motive which can be assigned for their disposition to manifest, the wish to make us wiser and better than we otherwise are.

Apart from these considerations of form and substance, the spirit hypothesis is at the stage of the inspiration-hypothesis above all superfluous, a fifth wheel to the cart. At the stage of the possession hypothesis spirit-co-operation seemed still indispensable only by reason of the supposition that the medium had no intelligence at his disposal besides his (either suppressed or displaced) waking consciousness. At the stage of the inspiration-hypothesis, this supposition no longer existing, it must first be inferred from the particular import of the communications that the medium's somnambulic consciousness was not able to produce it. As long as nothing is known of the hyperæsthesia of somnambulic memory, thought-reading, and clairvoyance, all those communications pass for revelations of inspiring spirits, which show an ideal content foreign to the waking conscious-ness of the medium, or evidently so by way of his sense perception. As soon, however, as these three sources of knowledge besides sense-perception are conceded, there is generally no ideal content thinkable, which would be naturally incapable of derivation from them.

Spiritism, however, cannot dispute the possibility of thought-transference from one mind to others, and of clairvoyance, without cutting away the possibility of inspiration itself ; for what the inspiring spirit knows, it can only, failing organs of sense perception, have learnt by clairvoyance or thought-reading, and what the medium's somnambulic consciousness receives from this spirit, can only be received by inspiration, that is, by thought-transference. The interposition of the thought-reading (or clairvoyant) and inspiring spirit between the thought-reading (or clairvoyant) medium, and the ideal purport to be perceived is thus not a solution, but only a doubling of the difficulty inherent in the problem of thought-reading or clairvoyance, aggravated by the circumstance that for the reasons pointed out, thought-reading from the consciousness of a bodiless spirit is much more difficult for the medium than that from the thoughts of another man, especially one sitting by him and connected with him by direct or indirect bodily contact.

Thus has the whole spirit hypothesis resolved itself into a pure nothing, when first the direct physical force performances, then the production of materialisation phenomena, and lastly that of the ideality of the manifestations have been shifted from the supposed spirits to the medium. Whether there are spirits or not we have not here to inquire; at all events, they are relegated, if they exist, to that beyond, from which Spiritism thought to have drawn them down.

There are some general methodological axioms which are not to be trangressed with impunity. First, principles are not to be multiplied without necessity ; thus a second sort of causes are not to be supposed, as long as a single sort will suffice. Secondly, we should as long as possible abide by causes whose existence is guaranteed by experience or indubitable inference, and should not unnecessarily catch at causes of doubtful or unproven existence, such as are to be first established by their value as hypothesis for the explanation of phenomena in question. Thirdly, we should as long as possible try to do with natural causes and not touch supernatural ones without urgent necessity. Against these three axioms Spiritism offends. The one, empirically given, natural sort of cause which we possess in the mediums it recognises indeed, but along with that it sets up a second, not empirically given, supernatural sort of cause, the existence of which is to be proved for the first time by this phenomenal province in question.

Now in order that with the first sort of cause we should allow the second also to avail, Spiritism must feel constrained to apply its whole force to define exactly the boundary line, beyond which the explanatory power of the first sort of cause ceases, and to show with the most careful critique *why* its sufficiency ceases beyond this line. So long as this definition of boundary and this proof are not forthcoming, the burden of proof lying on the asserter of the second sort of cause is not discharged, but Spiritism has *not as yet made the least attempt* to acquit itself of this obligation. So long as that remains unfulfilled the spirit-hypothesis lacks any glimmer of scientific foundation and warrant, and all philosophers who have adopted the spirit-hypothesis of Spiritism have shown thereby a serious deficiency of critical circumspection.

FINIS.

APPENDIX.

———

[While this translation is in the Press, further reports of the phenomenon of stone throwing have come to hand from Belgrade, the police being wholly unable to obtain a clue, though the stones fell repeatedly before their eyes on consecutive days, in the open street. (*Neues Belgrader Tageblatt*, 6th, 7th, and 8th August, 1885, cited in *Psychische Studién* for September.)– TR.]